ZÜRICH
TRAVEL GUIDE

THE ULTIMATE POCKET ESCORT TO SCENIC SPOTS, AND FINEST THINGS TO SEE AND DO, FROM ICONIC LANDMARKS TO VIBRANT HISTORY, IN THE HEART OF SWITZERLAND, FOR FIRST TIME VISITORS

CHRISTINE M. EDMONSON

COPYRIGHT © 2023 BY CHRISTINE M. EDMONSON

All rights reserved. No part of this publication may be reproduced, distributed, or transmitted in any form or by any means, including photocopying, recording, or other electronic or mechanical methods, without the prior written permission of the publisher, except in the case of brief quotations embodied in critical reviews and certain other non-commercial uses permitted by copyright law.

This book, "Zürich Travel Guide," is an intellectual property of the author and represents the culmination of extensive research and firsthand experiences. The comprehensive information, insightful recommendations, and captivating narratives are intended to aid and enrich the travel experiences of readers seeking to explore the wonders of Zürich, Switzerland.

Any unauthorized copying, dissemination, or duplication of the contents within this book is strictly prohibited and may result in legal action. Respect for the author's work and adherence to copyright laws not only protect the rights of the creator but also encourage the production of more valuable and enlightening literary works in the future.

Thank you for your understanding and support in safeguarding intellectual property rights. Happy reading and safe travels!

ACKNOWLEDGEMENTS

Writing the "Zürich Travel Guide" would not have been possible without the joint efforts, support, and inspiration of various people and organizations that have contributed to this rewarding adventure.

First and foremost, I express my deepest appreciation to my family for their unfailing support, understanding, and patience during this writing process. Their love and trust in me have been my continual drive.

I am truly appreciative to my editor and publishing team for their useful assistance and thorough attention to detail, assuring the book's quality and coherence.

My admiration also goes to the people of Zürich and the different local experts, tourist authorities, and citizens who graciously volunteered their thoughts and expertise, making this book a real expression of the city's beauty and soul.

Lastly, I would like to convey my heartfelt appreciation to my readers, whose curiosity and drive to discover the globe have made this venture important and fulfilling.

With deep gratitude,

Christine M. Edmonson

Zürich To-Do List
Itinerary

Monday

Tuesday

Wednesday

Thursday

Friday

Saturday

TABLE OF CONTENTS

ACKNOWLEDGEMENTS	3
ZURICH UNWRAPPED: A TRAVELOGUE	9
HOW TO USE THIS BOOK	11
CHAPTER ONE	13
WELCOME TO ZÜRICH	13
ZÜRICH: A HISTORICAL PERSPECTIVE	13
KEY HISTORICAL EVENTS	17
ZÜRICH'S ROLE IN SWISS CONFEDERATION	19
MODERN DEVELOPMENT AND GLOBAL INFLUENCE	20
GEOGRAPHY OF ZÜRICH	22
CLIMATE AND WEATHER PATTERNS	24
WEATHER-RELATED TRAVEL TIPS	25
POPULATION AND DEMOGRAPHICS	26
CULTURE AND ETHNICITY	28
CHALLENGES ZÜRICH FACES IN TERMS OF ITS CULTURE & ETHNICITY	35
CHAPTER TWO	37
BEFORE YOU GO	37
ENTRY REQUIREMENTS AND VISAS	37
ELIGIBILITY & DOCUMENTS REQUIREMENTS	38
TRAVEL INSURANCE	40
VACCINATIONS AND HEALTH PRECAUTIONS	42
CURRENCY AND MONEY MATTERS	43

CHAPTER THREE — 45

PLANNING YOUR TRIP — 45

- WHY VISIT ZÜRICH? — 45
- WHAT TO EXPECT IN ZÜRICH — 47
- BEST TIME TO VISIT ZÜRICH — 48
- DURATION OF STAY — 49
- CREATING AN ITINERARY — 50
- SUGGESTED 7 DAYS ITINERARY — 51
- PACKING FOR YOUR TRIP — 54
- PACKING TIPS AND TRICKS — 58

CHAPTER FOUR — 61

GETTING TO ZÜRICH — 61

- AIR TRAVEL AND AIRPORT INFORMATION — 61
- GETTING TO AND FROM THE AIRPORT — 62
- ROAD-TRIP OPTIONS TO ZÜRICH — 63
- GETTING AROUND ZÜRICH — 65
- PUBLIC TRANSPORTATION SYSTEM — 65
- CITY PASSES AND TRAVEL CARDS — 67
- TAXI SERVICES AND RIDE-SHARING — 68

CHAPTER FIVE — 71

ACCOMMODATION IN ZÜRICH — 71

- CHOOSING THE RIGHT NEIGHBORHOOD — 71
- BUDGET-FRIENDLY AND LUXURIOUS HOTELS — 73

CHAPTER SIX — 85

DINING AND CUISINE 85

Zürich Culinary Delights 85
Popular Local Dishes 87
Best Restaurants and Fine Dining Spots 90
Dining Etiquette 95

CHAPTER SEVEN 97

EXPLORING ZÜRICH'S HISTORICAL LANDMARKS 97

Ancient Churches and Cathedrals 97
Contemporary Art and Theaters 109
Architectural Marvels & Historical Buildings 121

CHAPTER EIGHT 125

SHOPPING IN ZÜRICH 125

Renowned Shopping Districts 125
Luxury Boutiques and Designer Brands 127
Local Markets and Unique Souvenirs 138
Tips for Getting the Best Deals 155
How to Avoid Tourist Traps 157

CHAPTER NINE 159

NIGHTLIFE IN ZÜRICH 159

Lively Bars and Pubs 159
Trendy Nightclubs and Lounges 166
Music and Entertainment Venues 171

7 | Zürich Travel Guide

CHAPTER TEN — 179

OUTDOOR ACTIVITIES AND NATURE — 179

- PARKS AND GARDENS — 179
- LAKESIDE ATTRACTIONS — 186
- HIKING AND ADVENTURE SPORTS — 196
- DAY TRIPS AND EXCURSIONS — 213
- SCENIC SWISS VILLAGES — 213
- NEARBY HISTORICAL TOWNS — 218
- CASTLES AND RUINS — 223
- LAKE CRUISES AND MOUNTAIN ESCAPE — 231

CHAPTER ELEVEN — 233

SAFETY AND PRACTICAL TIPS — 233

- EMERGENCY CONTACTS — 233
- LOCAL LAWS AND CUSTOMS — 234
- STAYING SAFE WHILE TRAVELING — 236
- COMMUNICATION TIPS — 238
- BASIC GERMAN EXPRESSIONS — 239

CONCLUSION — 240

APPENDIX — 241

- USEFUL WEBSITES AND RESOURCES — 241

ZURICH UNWRAPPED: A TRAVELOGUE

So, I've been aching for a vacation beyond the regular, a trip that will sweep me away to a world of adventure and discovery. Zürich, Switzerland's biggest City!, enticed with promises of stunning vistas, rich history, and a dynamic cultural scene. There was only one problem: my budget was as tight as a vice, and Zürich was infamous for being an expensive vacation. Determined to make this goal a reality without going penniless, I went on a journey to discover Zürich on a budget.

My journey started with considerable study. I perused every Zürich travel book I could find, combed forums, and connected with other visitors who had successfully toured this wonderful city without emptying their pockets. One recommendation that kept recurring was to invest in a Zürich Card. This miraculous card gave unrestricted access to public transit, including trams, buses, and boats, plus free or cheap admittance to several museums. It was my golden ticket to traveling about the city with ease.

Another money-saving jewel I uncovered was the Swiss Travel Pass. This ticket permitted unrestricted travel on Switzerland's large rail network, including the efficient Swiss Travel System. With it, I could see the lovely Swiss countryside on day excursions from Zürich without paying additional transit charges.

Food was another area where I needed to be careful. Zürich's food scene is world-class, yet eating out for every meal might rapidly drain my wallet. To achieve a balance between appreciating Swiss specialties and conserving money, I opted for a combination of eating experiences. I indulged in local street cuisine like bratwurst and raclette at inexpensive stalls, enabling me to enjoy true Swiss flavors without breaking my wallet.

Accommodation was another riddle I had to overcome. While Zürich features exquisite hotels, I opted for budget-friendly hostels and guesthouses in the city center. This not only saved money but also gave me the opportunity to meet other tourists and exchange advice.

One of my most prized discoveries was Zürich's natural beauty, which was absolutely free to enjoy. I spent hours meandering around the quiet beaches of Lake Zürich, picnicking in lovely parks, and climbing the adjacent Uetliberg Mountain for panoramic views of the city and the Alps.

Zürich also astonished me with its variety of free cultural opportunities. I walked the ancient Old Town's tiny cobblestone alleyways, admiring medieval buildings and soaking up the city's vivid vibe. Many museums and galleries gave free admittance on specified days or during certain hours, enabling me to admire Switzerland's art and legacy without paying a dollar.

In the end, my Zürich experience was a monument to the power of meticulous preparation and ingenuity. I discovered that a restricted budget should never be a barrier to visiting a desired trip. From historic sites to hidden treasures, from budget-friendly eating to decadent experiences, I collected all the knowledge I could acquire, and I created this book to assist tourists like me, in knowing how to get about. Zürich, with its delights, was no longer a terrifying riddle but a tempting experience ready to be explored without breaking the budget.

As I went home with a heart full of memories and a wallet still intact, I couldn't help but grin, knowing that Zürich had taught me the skill of enjoying luxury on a budget, turning my dream into a reality. Join me on this amazing tour across Zürich, and together, we'll convert aspirations into reality.

HOW TO USE THIS BOOK

This thorough guide is meant to be your ultimate companion as you begin an exciting adventure to experience the delights of Zürich. Whether you're a first-time tourist or returning to this charming Swiss City, this guide will give you crucial information and great insights to make the most of your trip.

1. Easy Navigation: The handbook is arranged into chapters for smooth navigation. Each chapter focuses on a distinct facet of your journey, from historical insights to practical recommendations, helping you to access important information quickly.

2. Comprehensive Coverage: From the historical backdrop and cultural richness to practical guidance on lodging, transportation, and safety, this guide covers all you need to know to enjoy a pleasant and satisfying trip in Zürich.

3. Insider Tips: Look out for insider tips and suggestions, providing you with hidden jewels and local experiences that will lend a distinctive touch to your vacation.

4. Weather Considerations: Pay attention to weather-related facts, as it will help you pack wisely and arrange outdoor activities depending on the environment during your stay.

5. Itinerary Ideas: In "Chapter Three: Planning Your Trip," you'll discover proposed itineraries that cater to varied interests and lengths, giving you a starting point to design your unique exploration itinerary.

6. Must-See Historical Sites: In "Chapter Seven: Exploring Zürich's Historical Landmarks," explore historic cathedrals, museums, and architectural masterpieces that showcase Zürich's rich past.

7. Retail and Nightlife: Uncover Zürich's busy retail districts and active nightlife scene in the devoted chapters, "Chapter Eight: Shopping in Zürich" and "Chapter Nine: Nightlife in Zürich."

8. Outdoor Activities and Nature: If you appreciate the great outdoors, "Chapter Ten: Outdoor Activities and Nature" gives options for enjoying Zürich's parks, lakefront attractions, and adjacent day excursions to attractive Swiss villages and ancient cities.

9. Safety and Practical Tips: Prioritize your safety and educate yourself with local laws and traditions by referring to "Chapter Eleven: Safety and Practical Tips."

10. Language and Useful Phrases: For ease of conversation, "Language and Useful Phrases" gives fundamental German terms that will come in useful throughout your contacts in Zürich.

11. Conclusion and Sharing: As you wave goodbye to Zürich, remember to share your trip experiences with us and record treasured memories.

We hope our "Zürich Travel Guide" acts as your expert companion, unveiling the riches of this interesting city and guaranteeing a rewarding and pleasurable experience. Safe travels and enjoy your time in Zürich!

CHAPTER ONE

WELCOME TO ZÜRICH

Greetings, fellow travelers! Get ready to go on a captivating trip through time and culture as we visit the charming city of Zürich. From its ancient Roman beginnings to its modern-day worldwide significance, Zürich provides a compelling combination of historical treasures and contemporary charm.

Zürich is split into 12 districts. Each district has its distinct traits and communities, adding to the city's vast variety. To identify the districts on a location guide or map, you will normally find them labeled with their district numbers. The district numbers are extensively used in Zürich, and they are written as Roman numerals. Here is the list of the districts with their matching district numbers: Example, District 1 - Kreis 1... District 12 - Kreis 12...

Let's plunge in together and unearth the hidden pearls of this Swiss gem. Are you excited? Let's begin this fantastic journey!

Zürich: A Historical Perspective

Hello there! I'm happy to take you on a voyage through the historical viewpoint of Zürich, from its Roman roots through the Middle Ages. Let's journey back in time and experience the rich history of this interesting city!

From Roman Origins through the Middle Ages

Roman Origins (circa 15 BC - 400 AD)

Welcome to ancient Zürich! The Romans initially arrived here approximately 15 BC, building a military outpost known as "Turicum." The site, strategically positioned on the banks of the Limmat River and at the crossroads of vital trade routes, had a crucial influence in molding Zürich's destiny.

Over time, Turicum flourished into a thriving Roman town, equipped with temples, public baths, and an amphitheater. The residents worked in commerce, agriculture, and crafts, making it a vibrant settlement under the Roman Empire.

Middle Ages (approximately 400 AD - 1300 AD)

As we move to the Middle Ages, Zürich faced several obstacles. The collapse of the Western Roman Empire in the 5th century brought about a time of instability, and the territory fell under the control of several Germanic tribes.

Amid this volatile period, Zürich became part of the Carolingian Empire and then the Holy Roman Empire. The local ruling house, the House of Zähringen, had a vital part in the city's rise. They established Zürich's first city charter, offering the town major advantages, including market rights.

Zürich's position as a commercial center developed, mainly owing to its location along the trade routes of the Rhine River. By the 12th century, the city had enlarged its defenses and established itself as a key urban center in the area.

In the later Middle Ages, Zürich underwent a thriving age of cultural and intellectual progress. The building of the Grossmünster, a grand Romanesque church, and the formation of the University of Zürich in 1833 (though it may be dated back to the Carolingian era) were key milestones in the city's history.

The guild system also gained root during this period, influencing Zürich's social and economic framework. Guilds governed numerous trades, and its members contributed to the city's administration.

Renaissance and Growth
The Renaissance was a period of immense cultural and intellectual awakening that swept over Europe, and Zürich was no exception. Let's enter into this exciting voyage together, shall we?

The Renaissance in Zürich
The Renaissance, a period lasting approximately from the 14th to the 17th century, brought forth a revitalized interest in art, science, literature, and humanism. Zürich, located in the heart of Switzerland, played a vital part in this transformational age. During the revival, the city underwent a cultural and economic revival of its own, making it a center for invention and creativity.

1. Intellectual and Cultural Revival:
The Renaissance in Zürich was marked by a renaissance of classical learning and the restoration of old Greek and Roman beliefs. The foundation of Zürich's university in 1833 offered a venue for researchers and intellectuals to assemble, share ideas, and accelerate the city's intellectual progress. The institution swiftly achieved popularity as a center of humanist studies, spawning a generation of philosophers who emphasized reason and empirical investigation.

2. Art and Architecture:
The Renaissance saw a significant development in the city's architectural and cultural landscape. Zürich witnessed the rise of excellent painters and builders who took influence from the ancient world. Magnificent structures, embellished with elaborate facades and paintings, started to dot the metropolis.

The Grossmünster and Fraumünster cathedrals are prominent instances of this architectural renaissance, exhibiting spectacular stained glass windows and exquisite sculptures.

3. Economic Boom:
Zürich's geographical position, located on the crossroads of key commercial routes, played a vital role in its economic expansion throughout the Renaissance. The city's strategic location helped it to become a booming commercial hub for commerce and banking. The textile industry, in particular, developed, providing riches to the city and contributing to its cultural patronage.

4. Printing and Literature:
The creation of the printing press by Johannes Gutenberg in the mid-15th century ignited a literary revolution, and Zürich was not left behind. The city became an important center for the printing industry, generating a huge assortment of books and manuscripts. Notable personalities like Conrad Gessner, a Swiss naturalist and bibliographer, made substantial contributions to literature and science during this time.

5. Reformation Movement:
The Renaissance also coincided with the Protestant Reformation, which had a tremendous influence on Zürich. Huldrych Zwingli, a significant member of the Reformation, opposed the Catholic Church's authority and fought for religious reforms. His views gained popularity, leading to the formation of the Swiss Reformed Church, which became the dominant religious force in Zürich.

6. Scientific Advancements:
The Renaissance was a period of considerable scientific discovery, and Zürich made its mark in this arena too. The city's intellectuals contributed to improvements in medicine, astronomy, and mathematics. Paracelsus, a famous physician and alchemist, made breakthrough discoveries in medical knowledge during this time.

Key Historical Events

Let's look into some of the most crucial events in its history!

1. Early Settlement and Roman Influence
Zürich's history began with its early colonization by the Celts circa 500 BC. However, it was during the Roman period that Zürich acquired prominence as a strategic site. The Romans constructed a customs station here in the 1st century AD, known as Turicum. Some vestiges of Roman structures may still be discovered in the ancient town.

2. The Middle Ages and Guild System
During the Middle Ages, Zurich prospered as a free imperial city. In the 12th and 13th centuries, it became a member of the Swiss Confederation. The city's economy flourished via commerce, and its social structure was built around guilds. These guilds played a key part in Zürich's administration and growth.

3. Reformation in Zürich
One of the most crucial periods in Zürich's history was the Reformation in the 16th century. In 1519, Ulrich Zwingli, a Swiss reformer, came to Zürich and started preaching against the evils of the Catholic Church. His beliefs contributed to the removal of sacred art from churches and the establishment of Protestantism. This marked the beginning of a huge religious and cultural transition in the city.

4. Scientific and Cultural Hub
By the 18th century, Zürich had turned into a famous scientific and cultural center. The foundation of the University of Zürich in 1833 further reinforced its status as an intellectual powerhouse. Many outstanding minds, including Albert Einstein, studied and worked in Zürich during this time, adding to its reputation as a hub for innovation.

5. Industrialization and Economic Growth
Like many other European towns, Zürich experienced rapid industrialization in the 19th century. The city's textile industry played a vital part in its growth. The construction of rail networks and other infrastructure improvements encouraged trade and commerce, resulting in tremendous economic growth.

6. Switzerland's Neutrality throughout World Wars
Zürich and Switzerland as a whole managed to stay neutral throughout both World Wars, which was vital in maintaining the city's historical history and infrastructure. While other European towns endured damage, Zürich emerged from the wars largely untouched.

7. Emergence as a Global Financial Center
After World War II, Zürich witnessed tremendous economic expansion and grew into a significant worldwide financial hub. Its stable political atmosphere, solid banking traditions, and attractive economic environment attracted global firms, further strengthening its wealth.

8. Social and Political Movements
During the late 20th century, Zürich became a hub for many social and political organizations. The city experienced major action in areas like civil rights, environmental protection, and anti-nuclear rallies. These movements affected Swiss politics and policy and helped establish Zürich's contemporary character.

9. Cultural Diversity and Modern Zürich
In recent decades, Zürich has become a dynamic and diversified city, with a booming arts and cultural scene. It holds several festivals, art exhibits, and international events. The city's dedication to sustainability and quality of life has also earned it a reputation as one of the most livable cities in the world.

Zürich's Role in Swiss Confederation

Zürich is not just a gorgeous city with attractive scenery but also a vital participant in defining the history and politics of Switzerland. Let's dig right in!

Founding Member of the Swiss Confederation: Zürich had a crucial role in the founding of the Swiss Confederation. On August 1, 1291, delegates from the three founding cantons – Uri, Schwyz, and Unterwalden – convened at the Rütli Meadow to take an oath of mutual protection and cooperation. Zürich, while not part of the founding three, quickly joined the confederation in the early 14th century, extending its power and contributing to the stability of the alliance.

Reformation Hub: One of Zürich's most important historical events was the Protestant Reformation in the 16th century. Huldrych Zwingli, a Swiss religious leader, initiated the Reformation in Zürich, leading to the rupture of the Roman Catholic Church. This had a tremendous effect on the city's culture, politics, and education, and also pushed neighboring Swiss areas to accept the Protestant religion.

Political and Economic Powerhouse: Over the years, Zürich's political and economic power increased enormously. The city became a hub of industry, finance, and innovation, solidifying its position as Switzerland's economic engine. Its riches and influence attracted countless academics, businesspeople, and artists, further boosting Zürich's status as a cultural powerhouse.

Defender of Swiss Independence: Zürich played an important role in maintaining Swiss independence throughout the Old Swiss War and the Swabian War in the late 15th century. The city was in the vanguard of the war against foreign forces seeking to control the area, and its actions enhanced the Swiss Confederation's image of being a cohesive and robust state.

Neutral Ground for Peace Discussions: Throughout history, Zürich frequently functioned as a neutral ground for peace discussions between warring groups. Its reputation for impartiality and stability made it an excellent venue to organize diplomatic negotiations, leading to peace and settlement in many disputes.

Federal Capital and Modern Politics: Though Bern finally became the capital of Switzerland in 1848, Zürich remains an important focus for Swiss politics. It is the biggest city in the country and a vital actor in developing national policies and decision-making processes.

Cultural and Educational Hub: Zürich's rich cultural legacy and strong dedication to education have molded its status as a major intellectual hub. It houses major universities and research organizations, generating a culture of invention and inquiry that continues to affect the country and the globe.

Modern Development and Global Influence

Zürich is a lively and cosmopolitan city noted for great contributions to different disciplines. Let's get into the specifics!

Economic Powerhouse: Zürich is generally called the economic hub of Switzerland. It has evolved as a worldwide financial hub and is home to major international firms, banks, and financial organizations. The city's stability, good economic climate, and well-developed infrastructure have attracted enterprises from all over the globe. As a consequence, Zürich plays a vital role in the worldwide financial system, contributing heavily to the international economy.

Technological Advancements: Zürich's rise as a technical center has been spectacular.

The city is a powerhouse for innovation and research, with numerous famous universities and research organizations fueling cutting-edge innovations. Organizations like ETH Zürich (Swiss Federal Institute of Technology) have garnered worldwide prominence for their contributions to science and technology. Zürich's devotion to research and development has resulted in achievements in different sectors, affecting companies globally.

Sustainability & Green Initiatives: In recent years, Zürich has been at the forefront of promoting sustainability and environmental awareness. The city's administration and citizens are devoted to lowering their carbon footprint and developing eco-friendly legislation. Zürich's sustainable urban design, efficient public transit networks, and wide green areas have set an example for cities throughout the globe, prompting others to follow suit in their attempts to battle climate change.

Cultural Diversity and Arts Scene: Zürich's thriving arts and culture scene has also contributed to its worldwide impact. The city features various museums, galleries, theaters, and music venues, drawing artists and creatives from varied backgrounds. Zürich has been a center for cultural exchange, holding different international events and festivals that highlight art, music, cinema, and literature. This cultural dynamic has helped Zürich establish a distinctive character that resonates internationally.

Global Diplomacy and Peace Initiatives: Switzerland, with Zürich as one of its important cities, has long been recognized for its devotion to neutrality and diplomacy. The city accommodates various international organizations and is a site for peace discussions and diplomatic gatherings. Zürich's position in fostering peace and cooperation on the global stage has gained acclaim and esteem globally.

Influence on the Banking and Finance Industry: Zürich's prominence as a worldwide financial hub has had a considerable influence on the banking and finance sector.

Swiss banks are recognized for their stability and confidentiality, drawing customers and investors from throughout the globe. Zürich's experience in wealth management and private banking has contributed to the city's influence in influencing worldwide financial policy.

Global Business and Innovation Hub: Zürich's strategic position, along with its superb infrastructure and business-friendly legislation, has made it an appealing destination for entrepreneurs and startups. The city supports innovation via different incubators, accelerators, and tech parks, supporting a robust startup environment. As a consequence, Zürich has become a center for IT and business conferences, bringing experts and investors from diverse corners of the world.

Geography of Zürich

Welcome to the fascinating geography of Zürich! In this section, we'll explore how Zürich's strategic location on the northern shores of Lake Zürich, nestled amidst the Swiss Alps, has shaped its identity as a vibrant and picturesque city. Let's embark on a journey through its diverse landscapes and captivating surroundings!

Location and Topography

Hi there! Welcome to our little chat about the beautiful city of Zürich! I'm thrilled to share all the exciting details about its location and topography. So, let's get started!

Location:

Zürich is a stunning city nestled in the heart of Switzerland, and it serves as the country's largest city and financial hub. It's located in the north-central part of Switzerland, right at the picturesque northwestern tip of Lake Zürich.

The city's geographical coordinates are approximately 47.3769° N latitude and 8.5417° E longitude. The city is surrounded by picturesque hills and mountains, making it a truly picturesque location.

Topography:
Zürich boasts a diverse and captivating topography that blends harmoniously with the surrounding landscape. Here's what you can expect:

1. Lake Zürich: The city's namesake lake, Lake Zürich, is a mesmerizing glacial lake that stretches about 25 kilometers (approximately 15.5 miles) in length. The crystal clear waters of the lake provide a tranquil escape for residents and visitors alike. It's a popular spot for various water activities such as swimming, sailing, and even stand-up paddleboarding!

2. Limmat River: The Limmat River gracefully flows through the heart of Zürich, dividing the city into two parts: the eastern and western banks. You'll find beautiful bridges crossing the river, offering breathtaking views of the surrounding architecture and landscapes. In the summer, you can often spot people swimming or floating along the river, enjoying the refreshing waters.

3. Hills and Valleys: Zürich is surrounded by gentle hills and valleys that create a picturesque setting. To the west, the Uetliberg mountain stands majestically, offering stunning panoramic views of the city and the Swiss Alps beyond. The Pfannenstiel chain of hills lies to the east of the city, providing even more scenic beauty. On the eastern side, you'll discover Zürich Berg, a wooded hill offering a mix of beautiful villas, gardens, and parks. The area is known for its peaceful ambiance and is a favorite among locals for leisurely walks and picnics.

4. Green Spaces: Zürich takes pride in its abundance of green spaces and parks, such as the beautiful Zürich Botanical Garden and the expansive Zürichhorn Park. These spots are perfect for picnics, relaxing strolls, and connecting with nature.

Zürich's topography blends the elements of water, hills, and mountains in perfect harmony, creating a mesmerizing environment for residents and tourists alike. The city's layout, with its green spaces, urban centers, and historical landmarks, makes it one of the most sought-after destinations in Switzerland.

Climate and Weather Patterns

Zürich has a temperate climate, with warm summers and cool winters. The average temperature in July is 21°C (70°F), and the average temperature in January is 0°C (32°F). The city receives an average of 1,400mm (55 inches) of precipitation per year, with most of the rain falling in the summer months.

The weather in Zürich can be unpredictable, so it's always a good idea to check the forecast before you go out. However, as a general rule of thumb, you can expect to pack for a variety of weather conditions, including sunshine, rain, and snow.

Here is a more detailed breakdown of the climate and weather patterns in Zürich:

Spring (March-May)
Spring is a beautiful time to visit Zürich. The weather is starting to warm up, and the days are getting longer. There are an average of 12 rainy days in May, so be prepared for some showers.

Summer (June-August)
Summer is the warmest season in Zürich. The average temperature in July is 21°C (70°F), and the days are long and sunny. However, it can also be quite humid, so be sure to pack light clothing and a hat.

Autumn (September-November)
Autumn is a lovely time to visit Zürich. The weather is still warm, but it's starting to cool down. There are an average of 10 rainy days in September, so be prepared for some showers.

Winter (December-February)
Winter in Zurich can be cold and snowy. The average temperature in January is 0°C (32°F), and there is an average of 15 days of snowfall per year. However, the city is well-equipped to handle the cold weather, and there are plenty of indoor activities to enjoy.

The Foehn Effect
One fascinating weather phenomenon that occurs in Zürich is the Foehn wind. This warm and dry wind descends from the Alps and can cause sudden and significant temperature increases. It's like nature's own heater in the winter and can lead to some unexpected weather changes.

Weather-Related Travel Tips
Here are some weather-related travel tips for Zürich:
1. Check the forecast before you go: The weather in Zürich can be unpredictable, so it's always a good idea to check the forecast before you go out. You can find the forecast on the Swiss Federal Office of Meteorology website.

2. Pack for a variety of weather conditions: Even if you're visiting during the summer, it's a good idea to pack for some rain and cooler weather. The weather can change quickly in Zürich, so it's always better to be prepared.

3. **Wear comfortable shoes:** You'll be doing a lot of walking in Zürich, so make sure you wear comfortable shoes. The city is also very hilly, so you'll want shoes that can handle some elevation changes.

4. **Bring an umbrella:** Even if it's not raining when you leave your hotel, it's always a good idea to bring an umbrella. The weather can change quickly in Zürich, and you don't want to be caught in the rain without one.

5. **Dress in layers:** This will allow you to adjust your clothing as the weather changes. If it's warm outside, you can take off a layer. If it's cold, you can add a layer.

6. **Be prepared for snow in the winter:** If you're visiting Zürich in the winter, be prepared for snow. The city gets an average of 15 days of snowfall per year. If you're planning on doing any outdoor activities, be sure to pack warm clothes and boots.

The Swiss Federal Office of Meteorology Website
The Swiss Federal Office of Meteorology (MeteoSwiss) is the national weather service of Switzerland. It provides weather forecasts, warnings, and climate data for Switzerland and the surrounding region.

The MeteoSwiss website is available in English, French, German, Italian, and Romansh. You can access it at the following link: https://www.meteoswiss.admin.ch/

Population and Demographics

There is a distinction between Zürich and the Zürich agglomeration, and what divides them is that Zürich is the city itself, while the Zürich agglomeration is the greater metropolitan region that encompasses Zürich and its neighboring towns and villages.

Zürich is a municipality in the Zürich agglomeration. The Zürich agglomeration is made up of 181 municipalities, including Zürich, Winterthur, Uster, and Dietikon. The Zürich agglomeration has a population of around 1.4 million people. Zürich is the biggest municipality in the Zürich agglomeration, with a population of roughly 434,000 inhabitants.

The Zürich agglomeration is a prominent economic and cultural hub in Switzerland. It is home to numerous multinational enterprises and organizations, and it is a major tourist destination. The Zürich agglomeration is also a significant transportation center, with Zürich Airport being the biggest airport in Switzerland.

Zürich's Resident Profile
Zurich is a varied city with a population of approximately 1.4 million inhabitants. The bulk of the citizens are Swiss, but there is also a considerable immigrant community, making up around 25% of the city's overall population. The most frequent foreign nationalities in Zürich are Italian, German, and Portuguese. The city also has a strong Turkish and Swiss-Italian community.

The average age of a Zürich inhabitant is 40 years old. The city boasts a well-educated population, with over 60% of the citizens possessing a university degree. The unemployment rate in Zürich is exceptionally low, at only 2%.

Zürich is a truthfully costly city to live in, yet it also provides a high level of life.
The city is home to numerous multinational enterprises and organizations, making it an excellent area to work. Zürich is also a famous tourist destination, with its gorgeous architecture, museums, and parks.

Languages Spoken
The official language of Zürich is German, although the major spoken language is Zürich German, the local variety of the Alemannic Swiss German dialect. You'll also hear English spoken regularly in Zürich, as well as Italian, French, and Portuguese.

If you're intending to visit Zürich, it's a good idea to learn a few basic German phrases. However, you'll also be able to get by with English in most locations.

Culture and Ethnicity

The culture of Zürich is a blend of Swiss and foreign influences. The city is home to a variety of museums, theaters, and opera houses, and it is also a prominent hub for the arts and culture.

Here are some of the major themes that I will discuss:
- The Swiss Culture and Traditions
- Influence of Neighboring Cultures
- Zürich's standing as a prominent hub for the arts and culture

I would also examine some of the issues that Zürich confronts in terms of its culture and ethnicity, such as the increase of xenophobia and racism. However, I would also underline the city's dedication to diversity and inclusiveness.

Swiss Culture and Traditions
Let's look into the unique characteristics that make Zürich a superb presentation of Swiss heritage:
1. Swiss Punctuality: In Zürich, time is respected, and punctuality is a way of life. The Swiss are recognized for their accuracy and dependability, and you'll find this mirrored in the city's fast public transit, well-organized events, and ordered everyday routines.

1. **French Influence:** While Zürich is located in the German-speaking zone, the French-speaking cantons of Switzerland are only a train ride away. The impact of French culture is quietly visible throughout the city, notably in sectors such as fashion and culinary arts. You could encounter French-inspired stores, cafés, and culinary delicacies that represent the beauty and sophistication of French culture.

2. **Italian Influence:** Zürich's proximity to the Italian-speaking part of Switzerland and Italy itself gives a touch of *la dolce vita* to the city. Italian food, with its savory pasta dishes and scrumptious pizzas, has surely made its way onto many restaurant menus in Zürich. Additionally, the laid-back and warm-hearted Italian culture has left a mark on the city's ambiance, making it more hospitable and appealing.

3. **International Business Hub:** As a worldwide financial hub, Zürich draws professionals and expats from all over the globe. This flood of numerous cultures produces a cosmopolitan environment, where various customs, traditions, and languages live happily. It's not unusual to hear languages from all corners of the world being spoken on the streets, reflecting Zürich's position as an international melting pot.

4. **Culinary Diversity:** Zürich's culinary culture is a reflection of its global background, inspired by surrounding nations and beyond. You may get a vast assortment of ethnic cuisines, from Asian delicacies to Middle Eastern pleasures and all in between. It's a veritable paradise for food enthusiasts eager to sample flavors from across the globe.

5. **Art and Design Fusion:** Zürich's art scene takes influence from both Swiss and foreign artists.
The city's galleries and museums present a varied spectrum of creative expressions, from classic Swiss paintings to modern pieces from artists throughout the world. This combination of creative ideas generates a dynamic and diversified cultural scene.

6. **Festivals & Events:** Zürich's cultural calendar is supplemented by adjacent influences. The city conducts several multicultural festivals and events, commemorating cultures from different nations. These events not only bring Zürich's citizens closer to their worldwide neighbors but also enable tourists to have a taste of diverse cultures without leaving the city.

The outcome of this blend of Swiss and foreign influences is a dynamic and diversified culture that is continually growing. Zürich is a place where you may enjoy the best of both worlds: the classic Swiss culture and the newest worldwide trends.

Art, Music, and Literature
Zürich's cultural landscape is a dazzling blend of art, music, and literature that embodies the city's dynamic energy. Renowned for its creative legacy, Zürich features a flourishing art community shown in several galleries and institutions. From historic Swiss masterpieces to cutting-edge modern works, the art scene provides numerous visual pleasures.

Music finds its beat in Züdiverse 's spirit, with a rich selection of concerts and shows spanning classical, jazz, and current genres. The city's famous opera house and music venues reverberate with tunes that stir the heart.

Literature flourishes in Zürich's intellectual milieu, previously home to renowned personalities like James Joyce and Dadaists. The city's bookshops, literary festivals, and public readings promote the written word, inspiring both inhabitants and tourists.

Together, these creative manifestations imbue Zürich with an aura of inventiveness, making it an enticing destination for cultural fans from across the world.
Celebrations and Festivals
Zürich is a city that understands how to celebrate life and culture, and its calendar is full of vivid festivals and events that bring locals and tourists together in exuberant festivity.

2. Classic Swiss Cuisine: Zürich's culinary scene proudly embraces classic Swiss meals, and one of the most renowned delicacies is the exquisite cheese fondue. Melted cheese, mainly Gruyère and Emmental, is offered in a communal pot, and guests dip slices of bread into the gooey pleasure. Another must-try meal is raclette, where raclette cheese is melted and scraped over potatoes, pickles, and cured meats. Swiss chocolate is also a culinary delicacy not to be missed!

3. Swiss German Language: The predominant language spoken in Zürich is Swiss German, a variety of the German language with its phrases and accents. While most Swiss Germans are conversant in standard German, you'll discover locals speaking their particular accent, adding to the cultural appeal.

4. Traditional Festivals: Zürich offers a range of traditional festivals that look into Swiss traditions and festivities. One such occasion is Sechseläuten, celebrated on the third Monday of April. It symbolizes the end of winter, with a procession of guilds and a ritual when the "Böögg," a snowman-like effigy, is burned on fire, signifying the approach of spring.

5. Swiss Watches & Clocks: Switzerland is recognized for its watch-making legacy, and Zürich celebrates this tradition with pride. You'll find various watch and clock stores around the city, showing some of the world's greatest timepieces.

6. Alpine impact: Zürich's closeness to the Swiss Alps has a profound impact on its culture. The enthusiasm for outdoor sports, such as hiking and skiing, is strongly ingrained in the Swiss way of life.
Even inside the city, you'll discover green areas, parks, and the lovely Lake Zürich, encouraging inhabitants and tourists alike to appreciate nature's grandeur.

7. Traditional Architecture: The architecture of Zürich nicely displays Swiss tradition. The old town, with its narrow cobblestone lanes and well-preserved medieval houses, oozes charm and history. The city's architecture smoothly integrates modernism with historic aspects, producing a distinctive urban environment.

8. Swiss National Day: On the 1st of August, Switzerland celebrates its National Day, and Zürich joins the celebrations with enthusiasm. The city comes alive with parades, fireworks, and different cultural activities, connecting inhabitants and tourists in the spirit of patriotism.

Immersing oneself in Swiss culture and customs while touring Zürich is an enjoyable experience. From relishing the delicacies of Swiss food to embracing the timeliness and charm of the inhabitants, you'll find yourself attracted by the genuineness and warmth that Zürich has to offer.

Influence of Neighboring Cultures

The impact of surrounding cultures on Zürich is a fascinating tapestry that gives even more liveliness to an already varied city. Let's discover how the adjacent cultures have left their stamp on Zürich's customs, traditions, and way of life:

On one hand, Zürich is home to several historic Swiss cultural institutions, such as the Swiss National Museum and the Kunsthaus Zürich. These institutions promote Swiss art, history, and culture.

On the other side, Zürich is also a prominent hub for international arts and culture. The city is home to several foreign embassies, as well as several international cultural institutions. This means that Zürich is continually exposed to new cultural influences from all around the globe.

Let's discover some of the most spectacular festivities and festivals in Zürich:

1. Street Parade: One of the most famous events in Zürich is the Street Parade, which takes place in August. This techno-music spectacle attracts thousands of party-goers from all around the globe. Colorful floats, decorated with vibrant dancers and DJs, march through the city, creating an electric scene. The Street Parade is not simply a music festival; it's a celebration of freedom, togetherness, and passion for music and dancing.

2. Sechseläuten: Held on the third Monday of April, Sechseläuten symbolizes the end of winter and the entrance of spring. The centerpiece of this traditional event is the "Böögg" burning ritual. An effigy of a snowman, signifying winter, is lit on fire as people excitedly await the moment when the head of the Böögg bursts. The earlier it occurs, the better the summer is projected to be.

3. Zürich Film Festival: Film aficionados celebrate during the Zürich Film Festival, held in September. This festival gathers actors, filmmakers, and cinema aficionados from across the world. The festival features a varied collection of films, including world premieres, documentaries, and avant-garde works. It's a fantastic chance to experience the magic of film in the heart of Zürich.

4. Züri Fäscht: Züri Fäscht is a major city-wide event that takes place every three years.
The events feature dazzling fireworks, music, street entertainment, and a myriad of food vendors serving a range of Swiss and foreign specialties. The event draws millions of attendees, making it one of the biggest public festivities in Switzerland.

5. Christmas Markets: As the holiday season approaches, Zürich turns into a winter paradise filled with dazzling lights and festive decorations. The city has numerous attractive Christmas markets, such as the Christkindlimarkt near Zürich's main railway station, where you can discover handicrafts, decorations, and delectable seasonal delights like mulled wine and roasted chestnuts.

6. Zürich Pride Festival: In June, Zürich celebrates its LGBTQ+ community with the Zürich Pride Festival. The city becomes a kaleidoscope of rainbow hues as parades, concerts, and cultural activities promote inclusion and equal rights. The event acts as a platform for promoting awareness and disseminating a message of acceptance and diversity.

7. Knabenschiessen: Every September, the Knabenschiessen festival combines a classic shooting competition paired with carnival rides and activities. Originally a tournament for young boys, it now includes females and young adults. The celebration generates a vibrant and pleasant ambiance in the city, with everyone partaking in the festivities.

8. Eidgenössisches Schwing- und Älplerfest (ESAF): While not held in Zürich proper, the ESAF is one of Switzerland's most prominent traditional festivities, taking place every three years. It's a Swiss wrestling and alpine event that draws athletes and fans from around the nation. Traditional music, yodeling, and alpine culture are key aspects of this great festival.

These are just a few examples of the various events and festivals that brighten Zürich's calendar throughout the year.
Whether you're a music fan, a film aficionado, a gourmet, or someone who values traditional culture, Zürich has something unique to offer throughout its countless celebrations. So, plan your vacation accordingly, and immerse yourself in the vivid and cheerful atmosphere of Zürich's festivals!

Challenges Zürich Faces in Terms of its Culture & Ethnicity

Zürich is an extremely varied city, with individuals from all over the globe calling it home. However, the city also has significant issues in terms of its culture and ethnicity. One problem is the increase of xenophobia and bigotry. Xenophobia is the fear or hate of immigrants, while racism is the notion that one race is superior to another. These views may lead to prejudice and violence towards persons of other cultures and nationalities.

Another problem that Zürich confronts is the assimilation of immigrants into Swiss society. Many immigrants come to Zürich in quest of a better life, but they frequently confront difficulties in integration, including language problems, discrimination, and lack of access to education and jobs.

Here are some incidents of xenophobia and racism in Zürich:
1. 2014: A group of black males were assaulted by a group of white men in the Zürich Old Town. The incident was purportedly motivated by racism.
2. 2015: A black guy was detained by police in Zürich after he was mistaken for a suspect in a crime. The guy was freed once it was evident that he was not the culprit.
3. 2020: A group of persons were assaulted by a gang of guys yelling racial remarks in Zürich. The incident was purportedly motivated by racism.

These are only a few instances of xenophobia and racism in Zürich. These instances still happen, but they are less prevalent than they used to be.

Despite these problems, Zürich is devoted to diversity and inclusion. The city has a variety of policies and initiatives in place to foster diversity, such as:
- A linguistic policy that encourages immigrants to learn German

- A program that gives financial help to immigrants who desire to create their enterprises
- A program that promotes cultural and social activities for newcomers

Zürich is also home to a variety of groups that promote diversity and inclusion, such as:
- The Zürich Integration Office
- The Zürich Diversity Forum
- The Zürich Intercultural Centre

These organizations aim to increase awareness of the value of diversity and inclusion, and they give help to immigrants and other minority groups.

If you are a visitor in Zürich, there are a few steps you may take to prevent becoming a victim of xenophobia or racism:

1. Be aware of your surroundings and be cautious of your conduct.
2. Avoid wearing apparel or carrying anything that might be viewed as provocative or disrespectful.
3. If you are approached by someone who is acting in a threatening or hostile manner, walk away and do not interact with them.
4. If you are the victim of a hate crime, report it to the authorities immediately.

It is vital to remember that Zürich is a safe city, and the great majority of people are kind and accommodating of travelers from all countries and origins. However, it is equally necessary to be aware of the possibility of xenophobia and racism and to take action to protect oneself.

The issues that Zürich confronts in terms of its culture and ethnicity are complicated, but the city is dedicated to resolving them. The city's policies and activities, as well as the efforts of the organizations that promote diversity and inclusion, are working to make Zürich a more inclusive and friendly city for everyone.

CHAPTER TWO

BEFORE YOU GO

Prepare for your vacation with critical pre-travel preparations. Ensure hassle-free travel by learning entrance procedures and visa laws. Safeguard your well-being with travel insurance and prescribed immunizations. Familiarize yourself with money, language fundamentals, and communication strategies to travel smoothly through your trip. Bon journey!

Entry Requirements and Visas

To enter Zürich, you must have a valid passport and a visa, if needed. The visa requirements for Zürich differ based on your country. You may check the visa requirements for your nationality on the website of the Swiss Federal Department of Foreign Affairs

Visas

If you are needed to obtain a visa to enter Zürich, you may apply for a visa at the Swiss embassy or consulate in your home country. The application procedure for a visa to Zürich might take several weeks, so it is advisable to apply well in advance of your intended trip.

Types of Visas

There are many sorts of visas available for Zürich, depending on your purpose of visit. Some of the most prevalent forms of visas for Zürich include:

1. **Tourist visa:** This form of visa permits you to remain in Zürich for up to 90 days for tourist reasons.
2. **Business visa:** This form of visa permits you to remain in Zürich for up to 90 days for business reasons.
3. **Work visa:** This sort of visa permits you to remain in Zürich and work for a Swiss firm.
4. **Student visa:** This sort of visa permits you to remain in Zürich and study at a Swiss university or institution.

Processing Time
The processing period for a visa to Zürich might vary based on the kind of visa you are seeking and the workload of the Swiss embassy or consulate in your home country. However, the processing period for a visa to Zürich normally takes several weeks.

Cost
The cost of a visa to Zürich varies based on the kind of visa you are seeking. However, the cost of a visa to Zürich normally varies from CHF 80 to CHF 170 ($93 - $200).

Eligibility & Documents Requirements

The papers necessary for a visa to Zürich differ based on the kind of visa you are asking for. However, some of the typical papers necessary for a visa to Zürich include:

1. A valid passport.
2. A visa application form that has been filled out appropriately.
3. Proof of travel insurance.
4. Proof of adequate finances to maintain yourself throughout your stay in Zürich.
5. A clean criminal record.
6. A letter from your work or school, if relevant.

Applying for a Visa

You may apply for a visa to Zürich at the Swiss embassy or consulate in your native country.

The application procedure for a visa to Zürich might take several weeks, so it is advisable to apply well in advance of your intended trip.

Contact Information

The Swiss embassy or consulate in your home country may provide you with further information about the entrance requirements and visas to Zürich. You may also find additional information on the website of the Swiss Federal Department of Foreign Affairs. Here is the website of the Swiss Federal Department of Foreign Affairs: https://www.eda.admin.ch/en

This website offers information on a broad variety of matters linked to Swiss foreign policy, including entrance restrictions and visas. You may access information on the website by clicking on the "Visas" tab. Here are the instructions on how to discover information about visas on the website:

1. Go to the website of the Swiss Federal Department of Foreign Affairs.
2. Click on the "Visas" tab.
3. Select your nationality from the drop-down option.
4. You will be brought to a website with information on the visa requirements for your nationality.

The website also contains a contact form that you may use to contact the Swiss embassy or consulate in your native country for further information.

Travel Insurance

Travel insurance is a sort of insurance that protects you from unforeseen events that may occur during your vacation, such as medical expenditures, trip cancellations, and lost baggage.
It is crucial to get travel insurance when you go to Zürich, as it may enable you to protect yourself financially in the case of an unforeseen occurrence.

Types of Travel Insurance
There are numerous forms of travel insurance available, so it is vital to pick the correct one for your requirements. Some of the most prevalent forms of travel insurance include:

1. Medical insurance: This sort of insurance protects you from medical expenditures that you may incur while you are traveling.

2. Trip cancellation insurance: This sort of insurance pays you for the expense of your trip if you have to cancel your vacation for a covered cause, such as sickness or a natural catastrophe.

3. Lost baggage insurance: This sort of insurance pays you for the expense of replacing your luggage if it is lost or stolen while you are traveling.

Benefits of Travel Insurance
There are several advantages to obtaining travel insurance when you go to Zürich. Some of the advantages of travel insurance include:

1. Peace of mind: Knowing that you are protected financially in the case of an unforeseen occurrence might assist you to relax and enjoy your vacation.

2. Financial protection: Travel insurance may allow you to protect yourself financially in the case of an unforeseen incident, such as medical expenditures, trip cancellation, or lost baggage.

3. Convenience: Travel insurance may be obtained online or via a travel agent, and it normally takes only a few minutes to apply.

Cost of Travel Insurance

The cost of travel insurance varies based on the kind of insurance you purchase, the duration of your trip, and your age. However, travel insurance is often extremely reasonable, and it may save you a lot of money in the case of an unforeseen catastrophe.

How to Choose Travel Insurance

There are a few things to bear in mind while buying travel insurance for your trip to Zürich. These include:

1. The sort of insurance you need: Make sure you get the correct form of insurance for your requirements. If you are just going to be vacationing in Zürich for a few days, you may not require medical insurance. However, if you are going to go hiking or skiing, you will need medical insurance that covers you for these activities.

2. The duration of your trip: The duration of your vacation will also affect the cost of your travel insurance. The longer your travel, the more costly your insurance will be.

3. Your age: Your age will also affect the cost of your travel insurance. Younger individuals often pay less for travel insurance than older folks.

Where to Buy Travel Insurance

Travel insurance may be obtained online or via a travel agency. When you are obtaining travel insurance, make sure you read the policy thoroughly to understand what is covered and what is not covered.

Vaccinations and Health Precautions

Vaccinations
There are no special vaccinations necessary for travel to Zürich. However, it is a good idea to stay up-to-date on your usual vaccines, such as measles, mumps, and rubella (MMR), diphtheria, tetanus, pertussis (DTaP), and polio. You may also want to consider being vaccinated against hepatitis A and B, as well as typhoid.

Health Precautions
In addition to immunizations, there are a few more health measures you should take before visiting Zürich. These include:

1. Staying hydrated: It is crucial to remain hydrated while going to any hot region. Drink lots of fluids, such as water, juice, and clear broth.

2. Avoid mosquito bites: Mosquitoes may spread illnesses such as malaria and dengue fever. Protect yourself against mosquito bites by applying insect repellent, wearing long sleeves and trousers, and remaining in well-screened locations.

3. Washing your hands: Washing your hands with soap and water is one of the greatest strategies to avoid the transmission of illness. Be careful to wash your hands regularly, particularly before eating and after using the restroom.

4. Dining safe food: When dining out in Zürich, be cautious to select eateries that sell fresh, prepared food. Avoid eating raw or undercooked meat, poultry, or seafood.

5. Be aware of your surroundings: Be mindful of your surroundings while you are traveling in Zürich. Avoid wandering alone in dark or lonely regions. If you are feeling unwell, get medical help immediately.

Currency and Money Matters

Currency
The currency of Switzerland is the Swiss franc (CHF). The Swiss franc is split into 100 centimes. The Swiss franc is available in the following denominations:

- Coins: 5, 10, 20, 50 centimes, and 1, 2, 5 francs
- Banknotes: 10, 20, 50, 100, 200, and 1000 francs

Exchange Rates
The exchange rate between the Swiss franc and other currencies changes, however as of now, the following are the approximate exchange rates:

- 1 US dollar = 0.86 Swiss francs
- 1 Euro = 0.95 Swiss francs
- 1 British pound = 1.11 Swiss francs

Where to Exchange Currency
You may exchange money at banks, currency exchange offices, and certain hotels in Zürich. The exchange rates at banks are normally the best, however, the hours may be restricted. Currency exchange bureaus are more handy, however, the exchange rates may be somewhat poorer.

Using Credit Cards
Credit cards are frequently accepted in Zürich. You may use your credit card to pay for most products and services. However, it is crucial to know that certain shops may levy a premium for credit card payments.

Using ATMs
There are ATMs all across Zürich. You may use your ATM card to withdraw cash from Swiss francs.

However, it is crucial to understand that your bank may impose a fee for ATM withdrawals.

Tips

Here are a few pointers for travelers concerning currency and money concerns in Zürich:

1. It is a good idea to exchange some money before you arrive in Zürich. However, you may also exchange money in banks or foreign exchange offices in Zürich.

2. Whether you are using a credit card, be careful to check with your credit card provider to see whether they levy a premium for credit card payments in Switzerland.

3. Whether you are using an ATM, be careful to check with your bank to see whether they impose a fee for ATM withdrawals in Switzerland.

4. It is a good idea to have some Swiss francs in cash on hand, particularly if you are going to be utilizing public transit or visiting smaller businesses.

CHAPTER THREE

PLANNING YOUR TRIP

Welcome to the fun time of arranging your Zürich journey! Discover why Zürich is an attractive place with its rich culture and gorgeous scenery. Get ready to immerse yourself in this cosmopolitan city, knowing the ideal time to come and planning your perfect itinerary. Uncover hidden jewels and must-see historical locations, guaranteeing an amazing tour awaits you! Let's plunge in together!

Why Visit Zürich?

Let me share with you the compelling reasons why Zürich should be at the top of your travel bucket list.

1. Rich Cultural legacy: Zürich possesses a wonderful cultural legacy that perfectly integrates tradition with modern art and architecture. Explore the picturesque old town with its medieval buildings, cobblestone streets, and ancient churches, affording a look into the city's history.

2. Spectacular landscape: Nestled between the magnificent Swiss Alps and the tranquil Lake Zürich, the city provides a spectacular natural landscape. Whether you're looking at the snow-capped mountains or enjoying a leisurely walk along the lake's shoreline, the magnificence of Zürich's nature will leave you entranced.

3. Cosmopolitan vibe: Zürich is a bustling and cosmopolitan city, drawing individuals from all over the globe.

You'll discover a melting pot of ethnicities, foreign cuisines, and a bustling arts scene. Embrace the city's uniqueness and feel at home in its inviting environment.

4. World-Class Shopping: For shopaholics, Zürich's Bahnhofstrasse is a wonderland. This premium shopping boulevard is home to high-end shops, known fashion companies, and fine jewelry stores. Indulge in retail therapy or browse unique shops for a shopping experience like no other.

5. Gastronomic Delights: Food connoisseurs will be charmed with Zürich's gastronomic delights. From the classic Swiss cheese fondue and raclette to worldwide gourmet eateries, the city caters to all taste senses. Don't forget to sample the wonderful Swiss chocolate, a genuine joy for your senses.

6. Cultural Events & Festivals: Zürich organizes a wealth of cultural events and festivals year-round. From the famous Zürich Film Festival to the vibrant Street Parade, there's always something spectacular going on in the city. Immerse yourself in the lively atmosphere of these gatherings.

7. Top-Notch Museums and Galleries: Art enthusiasts will be intrigued by Zürich's world-class museums and galleries. The Kunsthaus Zürich holds an excellent collection of Swiss and worldwide art, while the Rietberg Museum shows an unparalleled assortment of non-European art and antiquities.

8. Easy Access to Nature: Zürich provides a great blend between metropolitan life and natural beauty. With various parks, natural areas, and adjacent hiking trails, you can easily escape into nature while remaining in the center of the city.

9. Efficient Public Transportation: Zürich's efficient public transportation system makes it easy to explore the city and its surroundings. Trains, trams, and boats link significant destinations and make touring a breeze.

10. Kind Hospitality: Last but not least, Zürich's kind and friendly residents provide an additional touch of charm to your stay. Engage with the people, and you'll experience firsthand the real Swiss hospitality that will make your stay even more unforgettable.

What to Expect in Zürich

1. Zürich is a relatively pricey city: The cost of living in Zürich is one of the highest in the world. If you are planning on visiting Zürich, be prepared to spend a lot of money.

2. Zürich is an extremely clean city: The streets are clean, the air is clean, and the people are clean. You will seldom see rubbish on the streets, and you will never see anyone smoking in public.

3. Zürich is a highly secure city: The crime rate in Zürich is quite low. You can roam around the city at night without feeling afraid.

4. Zürich is a highly international city: There are individuals from all over the globe residing in Zürich. You will hear many different languages spoken on the streets, and you will witness people from various walks of life.

5. Zürich is a highly green city: There are several parks and gardens in Zürich. The city is surrounded by mountains, and there are numerous options for trekking and skiing.

6. Zürich is a highly cultured city: There are various museums, theaters, and opera houses in Zürich. The city also boasts a bustling nightlife scene.

7. The Swiss are highly punctual: If you have a meeting with someone in Zürich, make sure to arrive on time.

8. The Swiss are quite straightforward: They don't beat about the bush, and they are not scared to voice their thoughts.

9. The Swiss are exceedingly courteous: They will always say "please" and "thank you," even if they are simply purchasing a coffee.

10. The Swiss are highly proud of their nation: They will frequently converse about Switzerland's history and culture.

Best Time to Visit Zürich

Zürich is a wonderful city that can be experienced year-round. However, certain times of year are better than others for visiting.

1. Spring (April-May): Spring is a beautiful season to visit Zürich since the weather is beginning to grow warmer and the flowers are starting to blossom. There are also a variety of festivals and events that take place in Zürich throughout the spring, such as the Sechseläuten (a spring festival) and the Zürich Film Festival.

2. Summer (June-August): Summer is the most popular season to visit Zürich since the weather is bright and sunny. There are a lot of outdoor activities that you may enjoy in Zürich throughout the summer, such as swimming in Lake Zürich, hiking in the Swiss Alps, and visiting the various parks and gardens in the city.

3. Fall (September-October): Fall is a lovely season to visit Zürich since the leaves are beginning to change color. There are also a variety of festivals and events that take place in Zürich throughout the autumn, such as the Zürich Marathon and the Street Parade.

4. Winter (November-December): Winter is a lovely season to visit Zürich since the city is decked for Christmas. There are a variety of Christmas markets that you may visit in Zürich, as well as several other winter activities, such as ice skating on Lake Zürich and skiing in the Swiss Alps.

Ultimately, the ideal time to visit Zürich depends on your unique tastes. If you want to enjoy pleasant weather and outdoor activities, then summer is the perfect season to visit. If you want to experience the enchantment of Christmas, then winter is the finest season to visit. And if you want to experience a combination of everything, then spring or autumn are fantastic possibilities.

Duration of Stay

The length of your stay in Zürich depends on your interests and what you want to see and do. If you're interested in viewing the major tourist sites, such as the Grossmünster and the Kunsthaus Zürich, you may get by with a stay of 2-3 days. However, if you want to explore the city in greater detail, you'll need to stay for longer.

Here are some factors to consider while considering how long to stay in Zürich:

1. Your interests: What are you interested in seeing and doing in Zürich? If you're interested in history and art, you'll need to remain for longer than if you're only interested in shopping and nightlife.

2. Your speed of travel: If you prefer to take your time and see everything, you'll need to remain for longer than if you're satisfied to see the highlights and go on.

3. **Your budget:** Zürich is an expensive city, so if you're on a limited budget, you'll need to stay for shorter.

Here are some options for how long to stay in Zürich based on your interests:

1. **2-3 days:** This is enough time to view the major tourist sites and acquire a feel for the city.

2. **4-5 days:** This is ample time to explore the city in greater detail and visit some of the nearby places, such as Lake Zürich and the Uetliberg.

3. **6-7 days:** This is enough time to explore all that Zürich has to offer and yet have some time to rest and enjoy the city.

Ultimately, the best approach to determine how long to stay in Zürich is to evaluate your interests, your speed of travel, and your budget.

Creating an Itinerary

Start by determining what you want to see and do. What are your interests? What are the must-see attractions in Zürich? Once you know what you want to see and do, you can start to organize your itinerary.

1. **Consider your budget:** Zürich is an expensive city, so you'll need to include your money in your plan. If you're on a low budget, you may want to consider lodging in a hostel or guesthouse, dining at budget-friendly eateries, and utilizing public transit.

2. Think about your speed of travel: Do you want to take your time and explore everything, or are you glad to see the highlights and go on? If you want to take your time, you'll need to leave additional time for each action.

3. Be adaptable: Things don't always go according to plan, so it's crucial to be flexible with your timetable. If there's a museum that's closed for repairs or a restaurant that's out of your budget, be prepared to change your plans.

4. Leave some time for unanticipated activities: One of the nicest things about traveling is the unexpected encounters you have. Leave some time in your program for unexpected activities, such as meandering about the city and uncovering hidden treasures.

Suggested 7 Days Itinerary

Here's a 7-day scheme for a trip to Zurich, Switzerland, including morning, afternoon, and evening activities for each day:

Day 1: Explore Old Town (Altstadt)

Morning:
- Start your day with a visit to Grossmünster, a historic Zurich church. Climb the tower for magnificent city views.
- Explore St. Peter's Church and its iconic clock face, one of the biggest in Europe.

Afternoon:
- Enjoy a Swiss meal in a quiet café in the Niederdorf section of Old Town.
- Visit the Swiss National Museum to learn about Switzerland's history and culture.

Night:
- Dine at a typical Swiss restaurant for a fondue supper in the heart of Old Town.
- Take a leisurely walk along the Limmat River promenade.

Day 2: Lake Zurich and Parks

Morning:
- Start your day with a leisurely boat trip on Lake Zurich, admiring the gorgeous views.

Afternoon:
- Have a picnic at the magnificent Zurich Botanical Garden.
- Explore the neighboring Chinese Garden for a tranquil respite.

Night:
- Enjoy a lakeside supper at one of the numerous restaurants around Lake Zurich.

Day 3: Art and Museums

Morning:
- Visit Kunsthaus Zurich to explore its enormous art collection, featuring works by Swiss and international artists.

Afternoon:
- Have lunch in the museum's café or a nearby restaurant.
- Explore the Swiss Museum of Transport for a fun and engaging experience.

Night:

- Dine in Zurich-West, a fashionable area recognized for its bustling food scene.

Day 4: Day Trip to Lucerne

Morning:
- Take a train to Lucerne, a gorgeous Swiss town surrounded by mountains.

Afternoon:
- Explore the lovely Old Town, stroll over the Chapel Bridge (Kapellbrücke), and view the Lion Monument.

Night:
- Enjoy a Swiss meal at a restaurant overlooking Lake Lucerne before returning to Zurich.

Day 5: Zurich's Modern Side

Morning:
- Visit the Swiss Reformed Church and its magnificent stained glass windows built by Marc Chagall.

Afternoon:
- Have lunch in Zurich-West and visit its chic shops and galleries.
- Visit the FIFA World Football Museum if you're a soccer aficionado.

Night:
- Dine at a stylish restaurant in Zurich-West.

Day 6: Zurich Zoo and Uetliberg Mountain

Morning:
- Spend your morning at Zurich Zoo, home to a broad selection of species from throughout the globe.

Afternoon:
- Have lunch at the zoo's café or travel back to Zurich-West for eating alternatives.
- Hike or take a train to Uetliberg Mountain for panoramic views of Zurich and the Alps.

Night:
- Enjoy a nice supper at a restaurant in Uetliberg.

Day 7: Shopping and Farewell

Morning:
- Explore Bahnhofstrasse, one of the world's most prestigious retail avenues, for some last-minute shopping.

Afternoon:
- Savor a delicious lunch at a fine dining restaurant in the city center.

Night:
- Have a goodbye meal at a restaurant of your choosing, possibly revisiting a favorite site from your vacation.

This schedule delivers a combination of cultural, environmental, and gastronomic activities to make the most of your week in Zurich. Adjust it as required to meet your interests and speed. Enjoy your holiday!

Packing for Your Trip

Ready to start on a flawless travel experience? Let's guarantee you pack carefully! Explore weather concerns to dress accordingly. Discover the appropriate apparel and footwear to complement your trips. Don't forget those crucial travel essentials! Plus, discover packing tips and tactics to optimize space and remain organized. Let's begin packing!

Clothing and Footwear

No matter what time of year you visit Zürich, there are a few basic things that you should pack:

- **Comfy walking shoes:** You'll be doing a lot of walking in Zürich, so make sure you have comfy shoes.

- **Rain gear:** Even if you're traveling in the summer, there's always a potential for rain. Pack a raincoat and umbrella just in case.
- **Warm clothes:** If you're coming in the winter, bring warm layers, such as a jacket, scarf, and cap.
- **Hat:** A hat is necessary for keeping your head warm in the winter, and shielding you from the sun in the summer.
- **Sunscreen:** The sun may be intense in Zürich, even in the winter. Pack sunscreen to protect your skin.
- **Lip balm:** Your lips might grow chapped in the cold weather. Pack lip balm to keep them moistened.

If you intend to perform any outside activities, bring proper attire. This might be hiking trousers, a rain jacket, or a bikini. Don't forget to bring some good outfits for heading out. Zürich has a busy nightlife culture, so you'll want to bring some beautiful clothing for heading out to dinner or the clubs.

Travel Essentials
Here are some travel needs for a trip to Zürich other than clothing and footwear:

1. Passport and visa: You will need your passport and visa to enter Zürich. If you are not sure whether you require a visa, you may check with the Swiss embassy or consulate in your home country.

2. Travel insurance: Travel insurance is a must-have for every vacation, particularly if you are going to a foreign nation. Travel insurance will protect you in case of medical crises, lost baggage, and other travel misfortunes.

3. Money: Switzerland is an expensive nation, therefore you will need to carry adequate money with you.

You may exchange your cash for Swiss francs at the airport or a currency exchange bureau in Zürich.

4. Credit card: A credit card is a simple method to pay for products in Zürich. Most establishments in Zürich accept credit cards.

5. Sunglasses: The sun may be intense in Zürich, especially in the winter. Sunglasses will shield your eyes from the sun's beams.

6. Scarf: A scarf may keep you warm in the winter and shield you from the wind.

7. Water bottle: It is crucial to remain hydrated, particularly if you are doing a lot of walking. Bring a reusable water bottle with you so that you may replenish it during the day.

8. Toiletries: Pack your necessary toiletries, such as shampoo, conditioner, soap, sanitary wears, toothpaste, and toothbrush. You may also wish to include a travel-sized first-aid kit.

9. Book or Kindle: If you have any leisure during your journey, you may wish to pack a book or a Kindle to read.

10. Camera: Zürich is a lovely city, so you will want to carry a camera to document your moments

11. Power adapter: If you are coming from a nation with different electrical outlets, you will require a power adapter. Switzerland utilizes the same electrical outlets as much of Europe, therefore you can purchase a universal power adaptor.

Zürich utilizes the Type C power socket, which is the standard power outlet throughout Switzerland and much of Europe. The Type C outlet features two spherical prongs that are located 4.5mm apart.

If you are traveling from a nation that utilizes a different kind of power outlet, you will need a power adapter to use your electrical equipment in Zürich.

Here are some of the most common travel adapters for Zürich:

1. Universal power adapter: This sort of converter may be utilized in most nations across the globe. It is a wonderful choice if you are going to numerous countries on your vacation.

2. Swiss power adapter: This sort of adapter is particularly developed for Switzerland. It is a nice alternative if you are just going to Switzerland and don't want to lug along a big universal converter. Type J.

3. Combination power adapter: This sort of converter is a mix of a global adapter and a Swiss adapter. It is a wonderful alternative if you are going to numerous countries in Europe and want to have a single adapter that can function in all of them.

You can purchase power adapters at most electronics retailers or online. When purchasing a power adapter, it is important to verify the voltage and amperage specifications to make sure that it is compatible with your electrical gadgets.

Here are some extra data concerning hiking, swimming, and fishing necessities:

1. Hiking: If you intend to go hiking in Zürich, make sure to carry good hiking boots, appropriate clothes, sunscreen, bug repellent, and a hat. You may also wish to bring a backpack to hold your things.

2. Swimming: There are several lakes and rivers surrounding Zürich where you can swim. If you intend on swimming, make sure to carry a swimsuit, towel, and sunscreen.

3. Fishing: There are also numerous options for fishing in Zürich. If you intend on fishing, make sure to carry a fishing rod, reel, and bait. You may also want to bring a cooler to keep your catch fresh.

Packing Tips and Tricks

1. Pack light: Zürich is a relatively walkable city, so you won't need to bring a lot of baggage. If you're just coming for a few days, you can get away with bringing only a carry-on suitcase.

2. Pack for all sorts of weather: The weather in Zürich may be unpredictable, so it's a good idea to prepare for all sorts of weather.

3. Pack comfy clothing: You'll be doing a lot of walking in Zürich, so it's crucial to bring comfortable clothing.

4. Pack varied clothing: You can pack less clothing if you pack adaptable outfits that can be dressed up or down. For example, a pair of jeans may be dressed up with a lovely blouse or down with a t-shirt and shoes.

5. Pack for your activities: If you intend to perform any special activities, make sure to carry the right attire. For example, if you're going trekking, you'll need to pack hiking boots, a backpack, and other stuff.

6. Pack a reusable shopping bag: Zürich is a highly ecologically aware city, and many shops do not give plastic bags. By bringing a reusable shopping bag, you can help decrease waste and do your bit to safeguard the environment.

7. Carry a lock for your baggage: Zürich is a secure city, but it is always a good idea to carry a lock for your luggage. This will assist to avoid theft and keep your valuables secure.

8. Take a first-aid kit: Zürich has a solid public health system, but it is always a good idea to take a first-aid package in case of minor accidents. This can assist you to treat small injuries yourself and prevent having to go to the doctor.

9. Carry a copy of your passport: It is always a good idea to carry a duplicate of your passport in case your original passport is lost or stolen. This will make it simpler to acquire a new passport if required.

10. Take a list of emergency contacts: It is also a good idea to take a list of emergency contacts in case you need to get in touch with someone in case of an emergency. This list should contain the names, numbers, and addresses of your family, friends, and doctor.

11. Pack a daypack: A daypack is a terrific way to bring your basics with you while you're out and about in Zürich. Be sure to include your water bottle, sunscreen, sunglasses, and other necessities in your daypack.

12. Pack a travel pillow: If you're not accustomed to sleeping on flights or trains, a travel pillow might help you get a decent night's sleep.

Zürich Travel Checklist

DATE:
DESTINATION:

CLOTHES

BASICS

SHOES

TOILETRIES

ELECTRONICS

ACCESSORIES

OTHER

Important

CHAPTER FOUR

GETTING TO ZÜRICH

Let's dig into the intriguing methods of reaching Zürich and exploring this wonderful city. Discover the ease of air travel and valuable airport information. Unravel the mysteries of ground transportation alternatives, including the efficient public transit system, city passes, and travel cards. Don't forget about the simplicity of cab services and ride-sharing for flawless travel! Let's begin on this transportation journey together!

Air Travel and Airport Information

Airports in Zürich
Zürich has two airports:
1. Zürich Airport (ZRH): This is the major airport in Zürich and is situated approximately 10 kilometers north of the city center. It is the biggest airport in Switzerland and is serviced by most major airlines.
2. Bern-Belp Airport (BRN): This is a tiny airport situated approximately 20 kilometers south of Zürich. It is mostly used for private flights and charter flights.

Airlines that fly to Zürich
Most major airlines operate to Zürich, including:
- Swiss International Air Lines
- Lufthansa
- Austrian Airlines
- British Airways
- American Airlines

- Delta Air Lines

Flights from Various Countries
Zürich is well-connected to other nations, and there are direct flights from many major cities across the globe. Here are some instances of flights from various countries:

From the United States: There are direct flights from New York, Chicago, Los Angeles, and San Francisco.
From the United Kingdom: There are direct flights from London, Manchester, and Edinburgh.
From France: There are direct flights from Paris, Lyon, and Nice.
From Germany: There are direct flights from Frankfurt, Munich, and Berlin.

Getting To and From the Airport

There are a lot of methods to travel to and from the airport. You may take the train, bus, or cab.

1. Train: The train is the most convenient method to go to and from the airport. The S2 line travels straight from the airport to the city center. The trip takes roughly 10 minutes.
2. Bus: Several buses run to and from the airport. The bus stop is situated outside the main terminal.
3. Taxi: Taxis are accessible at the airport. The ticket to the city center is roughly CHF 60.

If you are a first-time visitor to Zürich, here are some tips:

1. Check the weather before you travel: The weather in Zürich may vary fast, so it's a good idea to check the weather forecast before you arrive.

2. Exchange your currencies for Swiss francs: Swiss francs are the official currency of Switzerland. You may exchange your money at the airport or a currency exchange office in Zürich.

3. Get a Zürich Card: The Zürich Card is a terrific way to save money on transit, sights, and trips. You may acquire a Zürich Card at the airport or a tourist information center in Zürich.

4. Be mindful of the Swiss tipping culture: Tipping is not expected in Switzerland, although it is appreciated. If you do decide to tip, a small amount is sufficient.

Road-Trip Options to Zürich

Here are some ground transit choices for first-time visitors to Zürich:

From the airport:
1. Train: The simplest method to go from the airport to the city center is via train. The railway station is situated in the basement of the airport, and it takes only 10 minutes to reach the city center. The price is CHF 6.60 for a single ticket.

2. Bus: Various buses go from the airport to the city center. The buses are a little slower than the train, but they are also cheaper. The price is CHF 4.60 for a single ticket.

3. Taxi: Taxis are accessible from the airport, although they are the most costly choice. The ticket to the city center is roughly CHF 60.

From other countries:
By rail, Switzerland has a good train network, and it is simple to travel to Zürich from other countries by train. There are direct trains from several important cities in Europe, including Paris, London, and Berlin.

Here are several direct trains from many major cities in Europe to Zürich:

1. Paris: The TGV Lyria offers direct trains from Paris Gare de Lyon to Zürich HB. The journey takes roughly 4 hours and 15 minutes.

2. London: Eurostar provides direct trains from London St. Pancras International to Zürich HB. The trip takes roughly 8 hours and 30 minutes.

3. Berlin: The ICE offers direct trains from Berlin Hauptbahnhof to Zürich HB. The journey takes roughly 4 hours and 30 minutes.

4. Milan: The Trenitalia offers direct trains from Milan Centrale to Zürich HB. The journey takes roughly 3 hours and 30 minutes.

5. Amsterdam: The ICE offers direct trains from Amsterdam Centraal to Zürich HB. The journey takes roughly 4 hours and 30 minutes.

These are just a handful of the numerous direct trains that go to Zürich from other major cities in Europe. You may find further information on the Swiss Federal Railways website. https://www.sbb.ch/en

By bus:
Various bus companies operate international bus trips to Zürich. Buses are a cheaper choice than trains, but they are also slower.

Here are several bus companies that operate international bus connections to Zürich from various major cities in Europe:

1. Flixbus: Flixbus is a German firm that provides low-cost bus services across Europe. They offer a vast network of routes, including multiple connections to Zürich from important cities like Paris, London, and Berlin.

2. **Eurolines:** Eurolines is a French firm that provides bus services across Europe. They have a long history of offering dependable and economical bus travel. Eurolines operates multiple connections to Zürich from major cities like Paris, London, and Amsterdam.

3. **Postbus:** Postbus is a Swiss firm that operates bus services across Switzerland. They also provide international bus connections to Zürich from important cities like Milan, Munich, and Vienna.

4. **Swiss International Air Lines (SWISS):** SWISS is the national airline of Switzerland. They provide bus services to Zürich from major airports in Europe, such as Frankfurt Airport, London Heathrow Airport, and Paris Charles de Gaulle Airport.

By car:
If you are driving to Zürich, you will need to pay a toll to enter the city. The toll is CHF 4.50 for a vehicle with one to four people.

Getting Around Zürich

Once you are in Zürich, there are various methods to navigate the city. The most common method is through public transit. The public transportation system in Zürich is quite efficient, and it is simple to navigate about the city by rail, bus, or tram.

You can also go to Zürich via cab. Taxis are quite pricey, but they are a practical alternative if you are traveling with a group of people.

Public Transportation System

I'm going to explain to you about the public transportation system in Zürich.

Zürich has an outstanding public transportation system, and it is quite simple to navigate about the city by rail, bus, or tram. The system is administered by the ZVV (Zürich Transport Association), and it is quite efficient.

There are various sorts of tickets that you may purchase for the ZVV system. You may purchase single tickets, day passes, or monthly passes. Single tickets are the most costly choice, but they are also the most flexible. The day permits are a wonderful alternative if you intend on doing a lot of touring in one day. The monthly passes are a wonderful alternative if you are staying in Zürich for a month or longer.

To purchase tickets for the ZVV system, you may buy them online, at the railway station, or through the ZVV ticket machines. You may also purchase tickets from the bus driver. However, this is the most costly alternative.

Once you have a ticket, you can just scan it when you get on the train, bus, or tram. The ticket machines will inform you which gate to travel through, and you will need to scan your ticket again when you get off.

The public transportation system in Zürich is quite straightforward to use, and it is a terrific way to move about the city. I suggest utilizing it if you are visiting Zürich.

Here are some extra recommendations for utilizing the public transit system in Zürich:

1. The ZVV website contains a lot of valuable information, including maps of the system, schedules, and ticket costs. ZVV-Website: https://www.zvv.ch/

2. You may also download the ZVV app on your phone. The app includes all of the same information as the website, plus it also lets you purchase tickets and plan your excursions.

3. If you are going with a group of people, you may purchase a group ticket. Group tickets are a cheaper choice than purchasing individual tickets.

4. If you are staying in Zürich for a long period, you may get a monthly pass. Monthly passes are an excellent method to save money if you are utilizing the public transportation system regularly.

City Passes and Travel Cards

Here are some of the most popular city passes and travel cards in Zürich:

1. ZVV Day Pass: This ticket provides you unrestricted travel on all ZVV public transit (trains, buses, trams, and boats) for 24 hours. It costs CHF 23 for adults and CHF 12 for kids.

2. ZVV 24-Hour Ticket: This ticket is comparable to the ZVV Day Pass, but it is only valid for 24 hours after the first time you use it. It costs CHF 21 for adults and CHF 11 for youngsters.

3. ZVV 48-Hour Ticket: This ticket enables you unrestricted travel on all ZVV public transit for 48 hours. It costs CHF 43 for adults and CHF 22 for children.

4. ZVV 72-Hour Ticket: This ticket enables you unrestricted travel on all ZVV public transit for 72 hours. It costs CHF 65 for adults and CHF 33 for children.

5. Swiss Travel card: This card offers you unrestricted travel on all public transportation in Switzerland for 3, 4, 8, or 15 days. It is a fantastic alternative if you intend on going to other cities in Switzerland than Zürich.

6. Swiss Half Fare Card: This card provides you with half-price travel on any public transit in Switzerland.

It is a wonderful choice if you are on a budget or if you intend on doing a lot of touring in Switzerland.

These are just a handful of the numerous city passes and transport cards available in Zürich. You may find further information on the ZVV website.
https://www.zvv.ch/zvv/en/home.html

Taxi Services and Ride-Sharing

Zürich is a highly walkable city, however, there are instances when you may need to hire a cab/taxi or ride-sharing service. Here's everything you need to know about both options:

Taxis

1. Taxis are a handy method to move about Zürich, but they may be pricey. The regular charge is CHF 6.50 for the first 750 meters, and then CHF 2.20 for every subsequent 200 meters. There is additionally a fee of CHF 2.30 for night trips (between 11 pm and 6 am).

2. There are several different taxi firms in Zürich, including YourTaxi, Zürich Taxi, and Taxi Zürich. You may hail a taxi on the street, or you can call one in advance.

3. If you're calling a cab, make sure to have the address of your location available. You may also ask the cab driver to suggest a decent restaurant or bar.

4. Tipping is not required in Zürich, although it is appreciated. A normal tip is 10% of the fare.

Ride-sharing services

1. Ride-sharing services like **Uber** and **FREE NOW** are a more inexpensive choice than taxis. They normally charge a basic cost, plus a per-minute and per-kilometer premium. The rates are frequently cheaper than taxis, particularly during off-peak hours.

2. To utilize a ride-sharing service, you'll need to download the app and register an account. Once you're set-up, you may request a ride by entering your destination. The app will show you the anticipated cost of the journey and you can watch the progress of your driver in real-time.

3. Surge pricing might occur during busy hours, so be careful to check the app before you request a trip.

4. Tipping is not required in Zürich, although it is appreciated. A normal tip is 10% of the fare.

Which is better?
Both taxis and ride sharing services are a wonderful method to move about Zürich. The ideal solution for you will depend on your budget and your demands.

1. If you're on a limited budget, ride-sharing services are a terrific alternative. They're frequently cheaper than cabs, particularly during off-peak hours. However, bear in mind that ride-sharing services might be more unreliable than taxis. The projected cost of the trip may fluctuate if there is surge pricing, and you may have to wait longer for a ride.

2. If you're searching for a more dependable solution, taxis are an excellent choice. They're always available, and you'll know the precise cost of the trip before you get in. However, taxis might be more costly than ride-sharing programs, particularly during peak hours.

Tips for utilizing taxis and ride-sharing services in Zürich
1. Make sure you know the fare before you get in the cab.
2. If you're utilizing a vehicle-sharing service, make sure to request a transport that is big enough for your group.
3. Be mindful of the surge pricing that might occur during busy hours.
4. Tip your driver with respect.

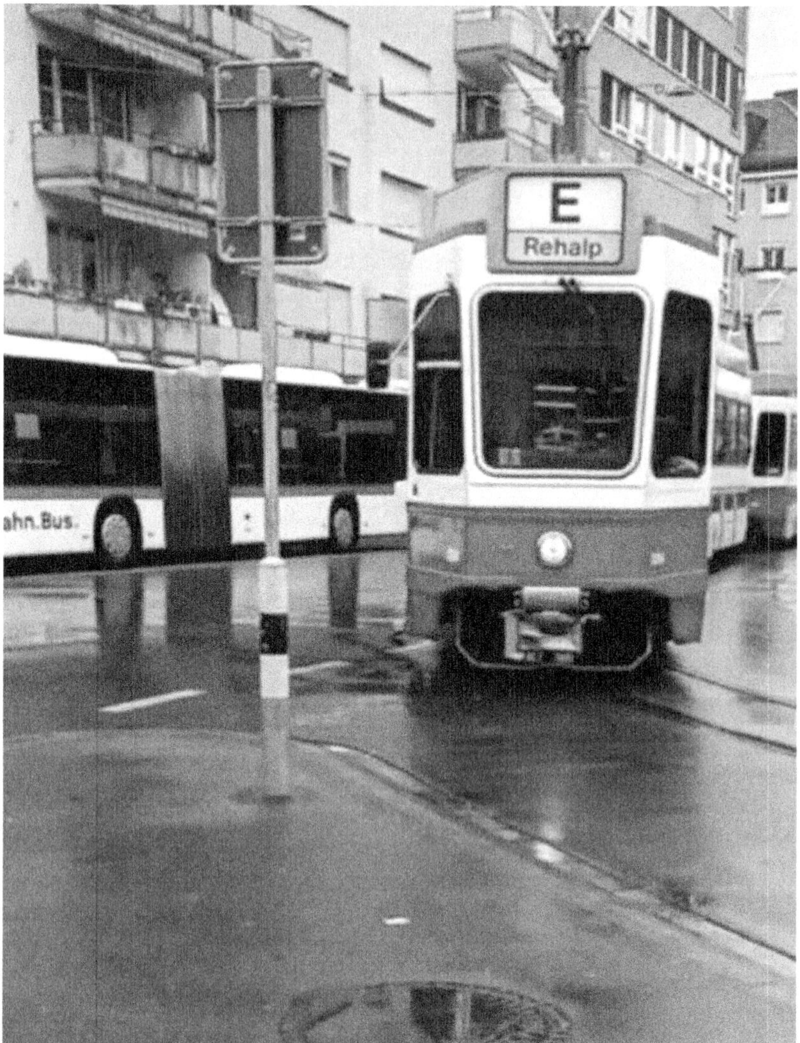
E
Rehalp
ahn.Bus.

CHAPTER FIVE

ACCOMMODATION IN ZÜRICH

Welcome to Chapter five of our tour to Zürich! In this chapter, we'll explore all you need to know about locating the right location to stay in this wonderful city. We'll discuss picking the proper location, the numerous sorts of hotels available, and booking advice and suggestions. So whether you're searching for a budget-friendly hostel or a deluxe hotel, we'll help you locate the right place to call home during your time in Zürich. Booking your accommodation in advance is suggested, particularly during the high season.

Choosing the Right Neighborhood

Zürich is a wonderfully diversified city, with something to offer everyone. There are many various communities to select from, each with its special character. So how do you select the appropriate one for you?

Here are a few things to consider:

1. Your budget: Zürich is a somewhat expensive city, so it's crucial to incorporate that into your budget when picking accommodation. Some communities are more costly than others, so be sure to do your homework.

2. Your interests: What are you interested in seeing and doing in Zürich? If you're interested in history and culture, you may wish to stay in Old Town. If you're interested in nightlife, you may wish to stay in Niederdorf.

3. Your transportation needs: If you intend on doing a lot of walking, you may choose to stay in a central area like Old Town. If you intend on taking public transit, you'll want to be sure that the area you pick is well-connected like Enge, Zurich West, Wiedikon, Sihlfeld, all in the Old Town (Altstadt).

Here are a handful of the most popular areas for visitors in Zürich:

1. Old Town: This is the historic center of Zürich, and it's home to many of the city's most prominent attractions, such as the Grossmünster church and the Hofkirche. It's also a nice area to roam around and explore the tiny streets and

Why it's one of the best:
If you're interested in history and culture, this is the area for you. You'll be able to view some of the most recognizable sites in Zürich, such as the Grossmünster church and the Hofkirche. You'll also be able to roam about the small alleys and lanes and get a sense of the city's history.

2. Niederdorf: This is the bustling, bohemian neighborhood of Zürich, and it's home to a variety of pubs, restaurants, and stores. It's a terrific spot to stay if you're searching for a dynamic and colorful environment.

Why it's one of the best:
If you're searching for a lively and active area to stay in, Niederdorf is the right neighborhood for you. There are usually people out and about, and there are plenty of pubs, restaurants, and stores to keep you amused.

3. Enge: This is a more expensive district, and it's home to several of Zürich's embassies and consulates. It's also a terrific spot to stay if you're seeking for a calm and tranquil area to unwind.

Why it's one of the best:
If you're searching for a calm and serene location to stay, Enge is a terrific alternative. It's a more upmarket area, so it's a little more costly than some of the other communities, but it's worth it if you're seeking a pleasant place to stay.

4. Zürich West: This is a former industrial region that has been turned into a fashionable and creative sector. It's home to a variety of taverns, restaurants, and stores, as well as several art galleries and studios.

Why it's one of the best:
If you're searching for a fashionable and creative location to stay, Zürich West is the right area for you. It's a former industrial region that has been turned into a dynamic and fascinating district. There are lots of pubs, restaurants, and stores to keep you amused, as well as several art galleries and studios.

No matter what your budget, hobbies, or transit requirements, there's a neighborhood in Zürich that's suitable for you. So take some time to conduct your research and choose the appropriate spot to call home during your stay in this wonderful city.

Budget-Friendly and Luxurious Hotels

1. Ibis cheap Zürich City West
GPS Coordinate: 47.3889729° N, 8.516186° E

Ibis Budget Zürich City West is a budget hotel situated in Zürich's famous Zürich West area. It's a terrific alternative for those who want to stay near the city's major attractions and yet save money. The hotel is only a short walk from the Technopark tram stop, which makes it convenient to move about Zürich. The hotel is 5 stories which contains 160 rooms non-smoking rooms, and 5 rooms for individuals with impaired mobility.

Check-in from 03:00 PM, and Check out up to 11:00 AM. German, Spanish, and English are the languages spoken at the hotel.

Here are some of the highlights of the hotel:

Location: The hotel is situated in the fashionable Zürich West neighborhood (**Technoparkstrasse 2, 8005 Zürich, Switzerland**). It's also a short walk from the Technopark tram stop, which makes it convenient to move about Zürich.

Affordability: The hotel is a wonderful alternative for budget-minded guests. It provides clean and pleasant accommodations, and it's still accessible to the city's major attractions. Price begins at USD 130.

Hotel Services: The hotel includes free Wi-Fi, a Car park, Air conditioning, and breakfast, which is an excellent value for the money.

Catering services: They offer a snack and beverage machine, with buffet service for an extra fee

Kid-friendly: It is children-friendly with services for children such as Children's TV Channels. It is also pet-friendly.

Excellent reviews: The hotel has excellent evaluations from past guests, which is a solid sign that you're going to have a pleasant stay.

Nearby landmarks:
Landesmuseum: It is around 2 kilometers (1.24 miles) away. It is a 30 min walk or 5 min driving
Opernhaus Zürich: It is around 5 kilometers (3.11 miles) distant. It is a 50 min walk or 15 min driving
Grossmünster: It is roughly 5 kilometers (3.11 miles) distant. It is a 1-hour walk or 10 min driving

Zürich Zoo: It is around 9 kilometers (5.59 miles). It is a 1 hour 30 min hike or 20 min driving
Fraumunster: It is around 2.99 kilometers (1.86 miles) distant. It is a 40 min walk or 10 min driving

Note: A COVID-19 certificate is needed inside, which proves a COVID vaccine or recovery as well as a negative test result upon admission into Switzerland.

Bookings & Reservation: h3184@accor.com
Telephone: +41 44 276 20 00

2. The MEININGER Hotel Zürich Greencity
GPS Coordinate: 47.2986° N, 9.5781° E

The MEININGER Hotel Zürich Greencity is a stylish hostel situated in the ecologically sensitive Greencity region of Zurich. The hotel is a 4-minute walk from Zürich Manegg railway station and is near the city center and Niederdorf Zürich.

This hostel is 14 minutes' walk from the Höckler hiking region, 4 km from the FIFA World Football Museum, and 6 km from the Kunsthaus Zürich art museum. It contains 174 rooms and 582 beds, 6 storeys and 3 elevators, 6 accessible rooms.

Free internet runs throughout the hotel and a gaming zone, lounge, and bar are available to rest after an energetic day touring the attractions. Restaurant Allegro (Italian restaurant), and Bürgli (Swiss restaurant), are nearby.

Smoking is not permitted in the hotel. **Check in time** is from 3 p.m. while **Check out** by 11 a.m. Late departure by 2 p.m. for only private rooms. German, and English are the languages spoken at the hotel.
City Tax: A local city tax of 2.50 CHF per person per night is not included in the price, to be paid at the reception.

Here are some of the highlights of the hotel:

Location: Maneggstrasse 41, 8041 Zürich, Switzerland

Affordability: The hotel is a wonderful alternative for budget-minded guests. Depending on the accommodation you pick, costs start from USD 135.

Hotel Services: Lounge, lobby, a contemporary bar with an industrial-chic ambiance, a communal kitchen, gaming zone, 24-hour reception, free Wi-Fi, parking garage (25 CHF per day, subject to availability), luggage storage (free), deposit boxes, vending machine, ticket service, washing & drying (for a modest price). There are no pools, hot tubs, exercise facilities, and spa.

Accommodation kinds: The hotel features a range of accommodation kinds, including mixed-sex and female-only dormitories, private rooms with en suite amenities, and family rooms. All rooms offer Wi-Fi, flat-screen TVs, and lockers.

Catering Services: Breakfast times: 6.30-10.30 a.m. Mon-Sun and public holidays.

Kid-friendly: It is children-friendly with services for children such as Children's TV Channels. It is also pet-friendly.

Website & contact information: +41 43 508 02 07
https://ww.meininger-hotels.com/en/hotels/Zürich/hotel-zurich-greencity/

3. Jet Hotel, Zürich Airport
Gps Coordinate: 47.4544° N, 8.5345° E
Address: Hofwisenstrasse 4, 8153 Rümlang, Switzerland

This calm 4-star rated hotel is a 4-minute walk from the Rümlang railway station, 5 km from the Zürich Airport, and 14 km from the Grossmünster Cathedral in the center of Zürich.

The sleek rooms are equipped with Wi-Fi, flat-screen TVs and balconies. The accommodation types include double and single economy, double room deluxe, triple room, double and single room business. Upgraded rooms have kitchenettes. Family rooms are available. It has no smoking policy. Pools and hot tubs are not available. It is child and pet-friendly, so come with your mini-mes and fur babies.
Check-in and out hours are 2:00 p.m. and 11 a.m. respectively.

Amenities: Free breakfast buffet and WiFi, kitchen in rooms, and parking (CHF 15), are offered. JET HOTEL serves coffee, tea, and water free of charge throughout your whole stay. There is availability of a bus transport to Zürich Airport for a charge of CHF 4.40.

Previous guests had appreciated the hotel for its nearness to the airport, its contemporary aesthetics, and speedy check-ins.
Contact information: +41 44 552 55 88
Website: https://www.jet.ch/

4. Hotel Baur au Lac (LUXURY)
GPS Coordinate: 47.36711° N, 8.53934° E
Address: Talstrasse 1, 8001 Zürich, Switzerland

Established in 1844, this stately, luxury hotel overlooks the Schanzengraben Canal. It's a 3-minute walk from Lake Zürich and 1.5 kilometers from the Swiss National Museum.

The hotel has plush, stylish rooms feature complimentary Wi-Fi and minibars, as well as TVs, DVD players, and marble baths. Suites include Bluetooth sound systems, and 1 has a balcony and a kitchenette. Some quarters offer canal views, and room service is accessible 24 hours.
Check-in time: 15:00, **Check-out time:** 12 pm. Prices start at USD 1200.
There are 4 high-end restaurants, 1 with a bar. A workout room boasts lake and mountain views, and there's a patio.

Parking, limos, and garage services are given for a cost. It is a kid-friendly hotel, and they provide babysitter services. It is a smoke-free home. Credit cards, Debit cards, NFC mobile payments, and Cash are accepted.

Amenities include; Air conditioning, free fitness facility, free Wi-Fi, and then Breakfast (at additional fee). At the fitness center, you have elliptical machines, treadmills, weight machines, free weights, massages, hairdressers, and doctors on call. There are no spas.

Services include; 24-hour front desk, baggage storage, concierge, full-service laundry, lift, wake calls, gift store, daily housekeeping, and turndown service. Parking & transport services comprise parking and valet parking at an additional price, electric vehicle charging stations, airport shuttle at an extra charge, private car service at an extra charge, and Local shuttle.

Kids & Pets: The hotel is Pet-friendly for an additional fee, and kids are permitted.

Languages spoken include Arabic, Cantonese, English, Filipino, French, German, Hindi, Indonesian, Italian, Mandarin, Portuguese, Russian, Spanish, and Vietnamese.
Contact information: +41 44 220 50 20
Website: https://www.bauraulac.ch/
Email Address: info@bauraulac.ch

5. The Dolder Grand (LUXURY)
GPS Coordinate: 47.3727°N, 8.5732° E
Address: Kurhausstrasse 65, 8032 Zürich, Switzerland

The Dolder Grand is a premium hotel situated in Kurhausstrasse 65, 8032 Zürich, Switzerland. It is set on a mountain top overlooking the city and Lake Zürich. The hotel was established in 1899 and has been refurbished multiple times throughout the years. It is currently a 5-star hotel with 179 rooms and suites.

It's a 4-minute walk from the closest funicular station and 2.3 kilometers from the Kunsthaus Zürich art museum.

A shuttle to central Zürich is free. The hotel features 2 restaurants and a seasonal dining deck, plus a lounge and a bar with live piano music. The spa provides an indoor pool, a gym, and beauty treatments.

The Dolder Grand is a favorite location for celebrities and other high-profile people. It has housed many renowned guests throughout the years, including Winston Churchill, Elizabeth Taylor, and Mick Jagger.

The hotel provides a lot of exquisite services, including sophisticated rooms offering free Wi-Fi, flat-screen TVs, and marble baths. Upgraded rooms include balconies with lake or mountain views, while the suites have whirlpool tubs. Some suites have living rooms and butler service, or saunas and balconies.

The rooms offer air conditioning, a kitchen in select rooms, a refrigerator, a coffee maker, and a minibar. the hotel features a spa, a fitness center, a sauna, a steam room, a swimming pool, and a rooftop terrace with panoramic views of the city. it also features many restaurants, a bar, and a cigar lounge.

The Dolder Grand is a popular option for **business travelers** and **vacationers alike**. It is positioned adjacent to several of Zürich's main attractions, including the Swiss Federal Institute of Technology, the Kunsthaus Zürich, and the Grossmünster Cathedral.

Check-in is at 3:00 PM and check-out is at 12 noon. Rates at the Dolder Grand start at roughly $900 per night for a regular room. Suites may cost upwards of $10,000 per night.

The Dolder Grand provides a range of amenities, including room service, laundry service, dry cleaning, and concierge service.
Telephone: +41 44 456 60 00
Website: https://www.thedoldergrand.com/

6. easyHotel Zürich West
Address: Dammstrasse 1, 8037 Zürich, Switzerland

This wonderfully pleasant but affordable hotel in Zürich is Located a short walk away from the lively Zürich West sector. Shops, cafés, and entertainment are all within an easy 10-minute reach, and best of all, you can enjoy these things on foot. Our modest hotel is a 2-minute walk from Zürich Wipkingen railway station, 2 km from the Swiss National Museum in the city center, and 4 km from Fraumünster Church. Prices start from $120.

Sitting pleasantly near the river Limmat and with Zürich Airport only 10km away, you can get from the aircraft to the hotel in about 20 minutes. From the airport, take the train S7 to Wipkingen (7 minutes). The station Wipkingen is located adjacent to the hotel. The hotel is a 20-minute walk from the main station. As a, the location could not be better suited to take advantage of Switzerland's fashionable and contemporary cosmopolitan attractions.

Nearby Attractions: Swiss National institution: This excellent institution is about a 15-minute bus ride away from easyHotel Zürich West Uetliberg: If you choose a trek, you may reach the bottom of the Uetliberg ascent with a 25-minute tram ride. Then you may climb for roughly 45 minutes to the peak for amazing views over the lake, the city & the Alps

WOW exhibition: This exhibition of illusions is a beautiful 30-minute walk away along the river from easyHotel Zürich West Fraumünster Church: You can reach this 11th-century church in approximately 20 minutes by tram.

Zürich Opera House: You can witness fantastic opera, ballet, and concerts at Zürich's Opera House, which is only 20 minutes away by tram.

Bahnhofstrasse: You can reach this busy retail area by jumping on the tram for a little under 20 minutes

Room Amenities: WiFi is accessible for free throughout the resort. There is heating. There are no air conditioning units at easyHotel Zürich West. They offer an En-suite bathroom with hair and body wash and fresh towels. Hairdryers and irons are provided at reception. Comfy Beds with a Cozy duvet and generous cushions. Room cleaning is provided at 25 CHF. TV is free to use.

Hotel Amenities: There are no parking facilities at easyHotel Zürich West. Baggage storage is free at the easyHotel Zürich West before you check in and after you check out, free of charge. There are no breakfast facilities, however, there are loads of wonderful food and drink alternatives nearby. Public spaces and wheelchair-accessible rooms are built to enable accessibility for wheelchair users and those with mobility issues.

Policies: Children are welcome as long as they are accompanied by an adult. An adult is regarded to be aged 18 or above. The easyHotel Zürich West enforces a strict no-smoking policy. They accept the Visa and MasterCard forms of payment. Check in time is 15:00, and Check-out time is 11:00. Please be reminded that you will be requested to present a new graphic identity upon arrival.

Payment options
Tourism Fee/City Tax: A required tax is levied by the city of 2.50 CHF per person every night. This is not included in the pricing and is due upon arrival at the hotel.

Contact Details: Email: Zürich_@easyhotel.com

Telephone: +41 43 322 05 53
Website: https://www.easyhotel.com/hotels/switzerland/Zürich

7. Oldtown Hostel Otter
GPS Coordinate: 47.3686°N, 8.5455°E
Address: Oberdorfstrasse 7, 8001 Zürich, Switzerland

If you are accustomed to staying in dormitories, you will love the central position with the option to have a fantastic night at the bar and meet many people - locals as well as other visitors. The tourist spots are all within walking distance from the hostel. The Lake of Zürich is about 200 meters away. The art museum and the opera house are just five minutes' walking distance and the famed Café Odeon is only around the corner.

The hostel provides 45 beds in the Oberdorfstrasse that passes through the upper section of the old town. It provides 9 dormitories and 5 individual rooms at affordable costs. There is a little kitchenette with a microwave, fridge, and oven to cook some modest cuisine. They provide complimentary coffee and tea in theirr common area accessible 24 hours. From 8:30 to 10:30 they serve some toast with jam/margarine and cornflakes/muesli with milk in the common room (self-service). Free baggage storage before check-in and after check-out is offered in a locker box in the common area on the 2nd level.

Unfussy mixed-gender or female-only dormitories have free Wi-Fi and bunk beds, plus lockers and charging stations. Linens are given, and restrooms are shared. Private rooms feature TVs; some have sitting spaces. Reception hours are from 8:30 – 10:00 and check-in 14:00 – 20:00. Check-in without a prior reservation is CHF 5.– extra per person/night. Check-out till 10:00.

Breakfast is provided. There's a guest kitchen with a microwave and a fridge and a café with a bar.
Contact information: +41 44 251 22 07
Email address: info@oldtownZürich.ch

Website: https://oldtownzurich.com/

8. Acasa Suites Zürich
Address: Acasa Suites Binzmühlestrasse 72 CH-8050 Zürich

Acasa Suites Zürich is a boutique aparthotel situated in the Oerlikon area of Zürich, Switzerland. The hotel is conveniently placed between Zürich airport and the city center, making it a handy alternative for both business and pleasure guests. It takes you 8 minutes to get here from Zürich airport if you're coming by vehicle. 48 Extra wide subterranean parking spots are ready for you. Charging outlets for electric cars are also accessible there. and if you arrive by rail, the train station Zürich Oerlikon is just 5 minutes on foot and frequent connections take you to Zürich Main Station and Zürich Airport in a 5-minute quick hop.

The Oerlikon district is a busy and up-and-coming sector of Zürich, with a mix of residential, business, and cultural activities. The hotel is within walking distance of the Oerlikon railway station, the Hallenstadion (a big music and sports venue), and the Messe Zürich (the city's convention center). There are also a variety of restaurants, pubs, and stores within easy reach of the hotel. They provide breakfast buffet or coffee from 7-9:30 am on Mondays through Fridays, and 7-11 am on Saturdays through Sundays, at an additional price of course.

The Acasa Suites Zürich provides a selection of large hotel rooms, suites, and serviced apartments. All of the apartments are contemporary and attractive, and several of them offer kitchenettes. The hotel also features a fitness facility, a spa, and a restaurant. They have an urban bar, lounge, and library to keep you feeling wonderful anytime. The apartment hotel also provides rooms for business meetings, so if you're traveling to Zürich on a business trip, you may make your booking there. Prices there start at $270.

E-Mail: welcome@acasasuites.com

Phone: +41 44 552 78 78
Website and Bookings:
https://acasasuites.com/en/acasa-suites-Zürich.html

9. Lamira Serviced Apartments
Address: Soodstrasse 22, 8041 Zürich, Kreis 2, Switzerland

Idyllically positioned at the foot of the Uetliberg, in the Sihl Valley are the serviced apartments of Lamira. The 20 completely equipped and furnished contemporary flats are located across four stories. They are excellent for anybody planning a short or lengthy visit to Zürich and the surrounding region. The Leimbach railway and bus station is approximately a 2-minute walk away. By automobile, you can reach Zürich's city center in less than 20 minutes. Prices begin at $180 per night.

The minimum days you may spend there is 3 days, and all their apartments offer an equipped kitchen, living, sleeping, and eating space, TV, FREE WiFi, as well as separate bathrooms. You may hire your parking spots for a daily cost. The building has a non-smoking policy, but you may only do it outdoors. Pets are accepted, at an additional fee. They have a separate sports and health center situated in the basement of Lamira.

The Lamira Serviced Apartments complex features a variety of services, including a laundry facility, a fitness center, and a sauna. There is also a garden with a BBQ area.

The flats are situated in a calm and serene region, surrounded by nature. However, they are also near a lot of stores, restaurants, and pubs.

Phone: +41 77 448 79 97
Email Address: info@lamira-zuerich.ch
Website: https://lamira-zuerich.ch/en/

CHAPTER SIX

DINING AND CUISINE

Get ready to tickle your taste buds as we dig into the realm of Swiss Culinary Delights, examining the nation's rich culinary legacy. Discover the spirit of Switzerland via its Popular Local Dishes and embrace the etiquette of Restaurants and dining to cherish every moment.

Zürich Culinary Delights

As a culinary connoisseur and lover of food, particularly Swiss cuisine, I can confirm that this bustling city provides a diversity of exquisite gourmet experiences that appeal to all palates. Zürich's culinary culture flawlessly integrates history with innovation, making it a delight for food lovers from all over the globe.

The essence of Zürich's eating experience rests in its various and great restaurants. From modest family-run eateries to high-end Michelin-starred venues, the city offers something for everyone. These restaurants not only exhibit classic Swiss foods but also provide foreign cuisines, reflecting the city's global character.

One cannot speak about Zürich's gastronomic wonders without mentioning its exquisite cheese fondue. The velvety-smooth combination of Swiss cheeses, frequently accompanied by freshly made bread cubes, is a timeless joy that draws people together in an environment of love and fellowship.

Swiss gastronomic pleasures extend to its drinks as well.

Wine enthusiasts may luxuriate in exquisite Swiss wines from vines tucked along the terraced slopes of Lake Geneva or the beaches of Lake Zürich. For those wanting a non-alcoholic choice, Swiss alpine herbal teas like Alpine Herbs or Melissa (lemon balm) give a pleasant and fragrant experience.

Another iconic dish that appears on the menus of many Zürich restaurants is "Zürcher Geschnetzeltes." This delectable delicacy contains thinly sliced veal in a creamy white wine and mushroom sauce, topped with crispy rösti - a typical Swiss potato dish.

Beyond the classic Swiss gastronomy, Zürich features a booming street food scene. The bright and busy food markets provide a diversity of alternatives, from gourmet burgers and exquisite kebabs to fusion dishes that merge tastes from other countries.

Zürich's gastronomic pleasures extend to its sweet offerings as well. The city is famed for its world-class chocolate, and you'll find various artisanal chocolate stores where you can indulge in the best Swiss creations.

For visitors wanting a taste of history, Zürich's old town has historic bars known as "Zunfthäuser." Here, you may sample classic Swiss meals in attractive surroundings that inspire a feeling of nostalgia and legacy.

Moreover, the focus on locally produced and organic foods adds an added dimension of freshness and sustainability to the culinary experience in Zürich. Farm-to-table restaurants and farmers' markets proudly highlight the region's abundance, enriching the whole eating experience.

Dining etiquette is an integral component of Zürich's culinary culture. Patrons are required to be prompt, courteous, and grateful for the chef's efforts.

It's normal to thank the employees while arriving and departing the institution, expressing appreciation for the excellent dinner.

In conclusion, Zürich's culinary pleasures provide a delightful voyage through Swiss traditions, current inventions, and foreign cuisines. Whether you're a passionate gourmet or a casual diner, Zürich's culinary scene guarantees to leave you with remarkable experiences and a better appreciation for the art of Swiss cuisine.

Popular Local Dishes

Zürich is a foodie's delight, with a broad range of eateries to pick from. But if you want to eat some genuinely traditional Swiss cuisine, here are a few meals that you should add to your list:

1. Zürcher Geschnetzeltes: This is a famous Zürich dish cooked with thinly sliced veal in a creamy sauce. It's commonly served with rösti, a Swiss hash brown, and a side of veggies.

2. Raclette: This is a melting cheese dish that's excellent for sharing. It's produced by cooking a wheel of cheese over a fire or grill, and then scraping off the melted cheese onto platters of potatoes, bread, and other accompaniments.

3. Fondue: This is another melted cheese dish, but it's served in a communal pot over a portable burner. You dip bread into the cheese using long-stemmed forks, and it's a terrific way to converse with friends and family.

4. Birchermüesli: This is a typical Swiss breakfast meal prepared of oats, yogurt, fruit, and almonds. It's a healthy and tasty way to start your day.

5. Zuger Kirschtorte: This is a delectable cherry dessert that's a specialty of the city of Zug.

It's constructed with a buttery sponge cake and a filling of sour cherries, and it's topped with a layer of chocolate ganache.

6. Cheese fondue: This melted cheese dish is a Swiss staple, and it's particularly popular in Zürich. There are many various forms of cheese fondue, but the most classic is created using Gruyère and Emmental cheeses.

7. Chesserli: These little cheesecakes are a favorite snack in Zürich. They're prepared with a flaky pastry shell and a filling of cheese.

8. Fondue chinoise: This fondue meal is produced with a variety of meats, vegetables, and shellfish that are dipped in a heated oil

9. Fondue au chocolat: This fondue dish is prepared with melted chocolate that is dipped in a variety of fruits, marshmallows, and other delicacies.

10. Mignardises: These little pastries are commonly offered after dinner in Zürich. They might be a range of various pastries, cakes, or chocolates.

11. Spätzli: These little dumplings are a favorite side dish in Zürich. They're commonly served with cheese or a cream sauce.

12. Rösti: This golden and crispy fried potato pancake is another renowned Swiss delicacy. It's commonly served with bacon, onions, and cheese

13. Zürcher Eintopf: Warm your spirit with a hearty Zürich-style one-pot stew including meat, veggies, and barley.

14. Kalbsbratwurst: Delight in the typical Swiss veal sausages, sometimes paired with mustard and a side of bread.

15. Swiss Chocolate: Treat yourself to the best Swiss chocolates available in varied tastes and textures.

16. Tirggel: Discover Zürich's oldest Christmas cookie, a spicy honey delight with exquisite motifs.

17. Zopf: Enjoy a soft and buttery Swiss bread braided into a lovely form, commonly served on Sundays. This braided bread is commonly served with butter and jam.

18. Nusstorte: Relish a delicious walnut tart with a flaky crust, that comes from the Engadine area.

19. Landjäger: Grab these dry and spicy beef sticks, excellent for a fast snack while visiting the city.

20. Älplermagronen: Try this Swiss macaroni and potato dish covered with cheese and topped with caramelized onions.

21. Chässchnitte: Delight in a cheesy Swiss toast toasted to perfection, sometimes served with a green salad.

22. Swiss Birchermüesli Ice Cream: Satisfy your sweet desires with this ice cream rendition of the classic Swiss breakfast.

23. Gespickt Hase: Embrace tradition with this seasoned and grilled marinated rabbit meal.

24. Maluns: Experience Swiss alpine cuisine with these shredded potato dumplings, commonly served with applesauce.

25. Buure Züri Gschnätzlets: Relish a farmhouse-style rendition of the popular Zürcher Geschnetzeltes.

These are just a handful of the numerous Swiss gastronomic pleasures that you may enjoy in Zürich.

So if you're in the city, make sure to taste some of these delicacies and enjoy the finest of Swiss cuisine.

Best Restaurants and Fine Dining Spots

Restaurants in Zürich are termed "Restaurants" in German. However, several additional words are used to define distinct sorts of restaurants. For example, a "Beiz" is a tiny, informal restaurant, whereas a "Kronenhalle" is a more premium place.

Here are some additional words that you could encounter while you're in Zürich:

1. Cafés: These are eateries that provide coffee, tea, and pastries.
2. Bistros: These are informal eateries that provide a range of foods, generally with an emphasis on local cuisine.
3. Tavernes: These are classic Swiss establishments that provide substantial cuisine and wine.
4. Speise Restaurants: These are restaurants that provide more formal dinners, frequently with an emphasis on foreign cuisine.
5. Gastropubs: These are eateries that blend the best of both worlds: wonderful cuisine and good beer.

1. Restaurant Kindli
Restaurant Kindli is a typical Swiss restaurant situated in the center of Zürich. The restaurant has been serving traditional Swiss meals for over 100 years, and it is a popular destination. The restaurant is situated in the Old Town of Zürich, only steps from the Grossmünster Cathedral.

Restaurant Kindli is the perfect destination for single travelers, business people, families, and friends. The restaurant offers a warm and friendly ambiance, and it is a perfect location to relax and have a tasty meal. The service at Kindli is unobtrusive, friendly, and attentive. The staff is courteous and knowledgeable, and they are always glad to assist you in finding the ideal food.

The menu of Restaurant Kindli contains a broad selection of Swiss cuisine, including cheese fondue, rösti, Zürcher geschnetzeltes, and Älplermagronen. The restaurant also features a decent assortment of foreign foods, such as pasta, pizza, and steaks.

If you are searching for a great and traditional Swiss lunch in a pleasant environment, then Restaurant Kindli is the right spot for you.

Location: Strehlgasse 24 CH 8001 Zürich, Switzerland.
Price range: Restaurant Kindli is fairly priced. Main meals vary from CHF 25 to CHF 50.
Reservations: Reservations are advised, particularly for dinner. You may book reservations online or by phone.
Website: https://www.kindli.ch/restaurant
Opening Hours: Kindli opens Tuesday to Saturday for lunch and dinner Kitchen from 11:45 am – 1:15 pm | 6:00 p.m. – 9:30 p.m. They are closed on Sundays, Mondays, and public holidays.
Telephone: +41 43 888 76 78
Email Address: restaurant@kindli.ch

2. Restaurant La Soupière

La Soupière is a fine-dining restaurant situated in the center of Zürich, Switzerland. The restaurant is based in the Hotel Schweizerhof Zürich, a historic hotel that was constructed in 1864. The neighborhood near La Soupière is named Niederdorf.

La Soupière is noted for its traditional French food, which is made by Chef Martin Fencz. The menu contains a range of foods, including foie gras, steak frites, and roasted scallops. The restaurant also features a broad range of wines, including both local and foreign wines.

The décor of La Soupière is beautiful and refined. The dining area is adorned with dark wood paneling and chandeliers.

The restaurant also features a private dining area that can be hired for special events.

La Soupière is a popular destination for both residents and visitors. The restaurant is available for lunch and dinner, and reservations are advised. La Soupière provides Dine-ins, but no takeout or delivery.

If you are seeking a distinctive eating experience in Zürich, La Soupière is a terrific alternative. The restaurant provides exceptional cuisine, service, and environment.

Location: Hotel Schweizerhof Zürich, at Bahnhofpl. 7, 8001 Zürich, Switzerland.
Website: https://www.hotelschweizerhof.com/en/dining/la-soupiere
Menu: hotelschweizerhof.com
Phone: +41 44 218 88 88
Opening Hours: They are open on Monday to Friday for Lunchtime from 11.30 - 14.30, and Closed on Saturdays and Sundays.

3. Alexis Restaurant and wine-bar

Alexis is situated in the center of the Old Town, only steps from the Niederdorf fountain. The restaurant has been in operation for over 20 years, and it's recognized for its wonderful cuisine, vast wine selection, and pleasant environment.

The cuisine at Alexis combines traditional Swiss meals with a contemporary touch. You'll find everything from fondue to Zürcher Geschnetzeltes to steak frites. This restaurant also provides steak, vegetarian, and seafood in a relaxed environment. The wine selection is similarly excellent, with over 100 wines from throughout the globe.

If you're searching for a special occasion restaurant, Alexis is a terrific option.

The dining area is stylish and sophisticated, and the service is superb. But even if you're simply looking for a casual dinner, Alexis is a terrific spot to sample Swiss cuisine at its finest. Reservations are advised, particularly for dinner. The restaurant is wheelchair accessible. They provide Dine-ins and Takeaway, but no delivery.

The dress code at Alexis Restaurant and Wine Bar is casual wear. This indicates that you should avoid wearing anything too casual, such as shorts, flip-flops, or tank tops. However, you also don't need to dress up too much. A great pair of trousers and a button-down shirt would be totally fine.

If you're not sure what to wear, it's always preferable to err on the side of caution and dress a little bit more formally. You'll feel more comfortable and you'll create a favorable impression on the other visitors.

Location: Niederdorfstrasse 40 Niederdörfli, Zürich 8001 Switzerland
Opening Hours: Mon–Thu: 11 a.m. to midnight, Fri: 11 a.m. to 2 a.m., Sat: 11 a.m. to midnight, and Sun: 4 p.m. to 11 p.m. They offer a Non-stop warm kitchen from 11:00 a.m. to 10:00 p.m
Menu: alexis-cana.ch
Phone: +41 44 252 37 88
Reservations: https://alexis-cana.ch/
Email Address: zuerich@alexis-cana.ch

4. Five Spice Thai restaurant

Five Spice is situated in the middle of the Old Town, only a short walk from Grossmünster. The restaurant has been in operation for over 10 years, and it's recognized for its genuine Thai food, pleasant service, and comfortable setting. It is simple to get to, just close to a tram station.

The menu at Five Spice provides a broad selection of Thai foods, from traditional favorites like Pad Thai and Tom Yum Goong to more innovative dishes like Massaman Curry and Khao Soi. The ingredients are all fresh and the tastes are wonderfully blended. Their cuisine is of outstanding quality and properly spicy. Prices are fair, though still on the pricey side if you've never been to Switzerland before.

If you're searching for a casual eating experience, Five Spice is a terrific option. The restaurant is modest and cozy, and the service is always pleasant and speedy. You'll feel like you're eating at a friend's house. The place is normally rather packed, thus reserving ahead is advisable on the weekend. They are open every day and also provide pick-up takeout & delivery service by their Thai courier.

Location: Sihlfeldstrasse 81, 8004 Zürich, Switzerland
Menu & Reservation: fivespices.ch
Phone: +41 44 291 00 42

5. The Krone Restaurant

The Krone has been in operation for almost 100 years, and it's recognized for its wonderful meals, welcoming environment, and friendly service. The restaurant is set in a wonderful historic structure that was originally constructed in the 16th century.

The cuisine of The Krone contains typical Swiss specialties, as well as some more cosmopolitan selections. You'll find everything from fondue to Zürcher Geschnetzeltes to steak frites. The wine selection is equally outstanding, featuring over 100 wines from throughout the globe.

If you're searching for a special occasion restaurant, The Krone is a terrific option. The dining area is stylish and sophisticated, and the service is superb. But even if you're simply looking for a casual dinner, The Krone is a terrific spot to sample Swiss cuisine at its finest.

Opening Hours: They are closed on Sunday. Monday through Friday, they are open from 9 AM to 11:00 PM, and Saturdays from 5:00 PM to 11:00 PM for dinner. Please note that the restaurant may shut early on holidays or special occasions. It is usually better to contact ahead to check the hours. (Hot kitchen opens from 11.30 a.m. - 1.30 p.m. and/or 6.00 p.m. - 9.30 p.m.)

Features: Gift cards available, reservations, outdoor seating, private dining, seating, parking available, highchairs available, accepts credit cards, table service, street parking, wine and beer, accepts American Express, accepts Mastercard, accepts Visa, digital payments, free Wifi, dog friendly, family style.

Cuisines: Swiss, European, Central European, Contemporary
Special Diets: Vegetarian friendly, vegan options, gluten free options
Meals: Lunch, Dinner, Drinks
Location: Badenerstrasse 705, Zürich 8048 Switzerland
Website and Reservations:
https://www.krone-altstetten.ch/online-reservieren
Email Address: krone@arbeitskette.ch
Telephone: +41 44 211 33 88

All restaurants online provide an English translation option, just in case you can't read in German or their native languages.

Dining Etiquette

Zürich is a cosmopolitan city with a diversified population, so you'll find that eating etiquette is a little more casual than in some other areas of Europe. However, there are still a few things you should keep in mind if you want to create a good impression.

Here are a few eating etiquette recommendations for first-timers in Zürich:

1. Be on time: Swiss people are highly punctual, thus it's crucial to arrive on time for your reservation. If you're going to be late, make sure to contact the restaurant as soon as possible.
2. Dress correctly: Most restaurants in Zürich have a dress code, so it's vital to dress correctly. This means no shorts, flip-flops, or tank tops.
3. Wait to be seated: Don't simply sit down at a table unless it's unoccupied and there's no one waiting to be seated.
4. Order your meal in German: This is a gesture of respect for the culture and the waitstaff. If you don't know German, attempt to learn a few simple words before you go out to dine.
5. Be nice to the waitstaff: Swiss people are highly nice, therefore it's crucial to be polite to the waitstaff as well. This involves saying please and thank you, and not making any demands.
6. Don't speak with your mouth full: This is considered disrespectful in most cultures, thus it's crucial to remember not to do it in Zürich.
7. Don't leave your napkin on the table after you're done eating: This is also considered disrespectful, so be sure to fold your napkin and place it on your chair after you're done.
8. Be mindful of the tipping culture: In Switzerland, it is traditional to tip your waiter or waitress roughly 10% of the cost.
9. Don't be hesitant to ask inquiries: If you're not sure what anything is on the menu, don't be hesitant to ask your waiter or waitress for an explanation.

These suggestions can help you create a positive impression on your next dining experience in Zürich.

CHAPTER SEVEN

EXPLORING ZÜRICH'S HISTORICAL LANDMARKS

Join me on a riveting trip through time as we unearth the mysteries of ancient churches and cathedrals. immerse yourself in the city's dynamic cultural scene with contemporary art and theaters. Let's dig into museums and galleries, where Zürich's rich history comes to life. and marvel at architectural marvels and historical buildings that stand as evidence of the city's intriguing legacy. Let's begin on this thrilling trip together! Are you ready? Let's go!

Ancient Churches and Cathedrals

Let's go on a trip through time and explore the secrets of Zürich's hallowed history. Are you ready to be fascinated by history's embrace? Let's plunge in!

A visit to the historic churches in the historic Town of Zürich normally begins with the Grossmünster, one of the most prominent monuments in the city. The tour guide will bring you through the history of the church, from its roots as a Benedictine abbey to its importance as the birthplace of the German-Swiss Reformation, and its participation in the Protestant Reformation.

You'll learn about the major personalities who had a part in the Reformation, such as Huldrych Zwingli and Heinrich Bullinger. Visitors may climb the towers of both the Grossmünster and St. Peter's Church for breathtaking views of the city.

The hike to the summit of the Grossmünster takes around 20 minutes, and the view from the top is worth it.

After the Grossmünster, the group will normally proceed to the Fraumünster, another lovely church in Old Town Zürich. The Fraumünster is famed for its Chagall windows, a set of stained glass windows that were made by the artist Marc Chagall in the 1960s. The windows represent biblical events and tales, and they are regarded to be some of the most beautiful in the world.

The trip may also include a visit to the Wasserkirche, a tiny church that is built on an island in the Limmat River. The Wasserkirche is notable for its Gothic style and its stunning views of the city.

If you're interested in learning more about the history of the Reformation, you may want to take a tour that focuses on this subject. There are a variety of guided excursions that cover the history of the Reformation in Zürich, and they often include trips to the Grossmünster, the Fraumünster, and other major locations in the city.

If you're searching for a more unique experience, you may choose to join a night tour of the historic churches in Zürich. These visits often take place after dark, and they provide a fresh viewpoint on the cathedrals. You'll see the churches lighted up against the night sky, and you'll hear about the history of the buildings in a more personal environment.

The Protestant Reformation in Zürich was a crucial turning point in the history of the city. It started in 1519, when Huldrych Zwingli, a priest at the Grossmünster, began to preach against the evils of the Catholic Church. Zwingli's views were popular with the people of Zürich, and he rapidly garnered a huge following.

In 1523, Zwingli and his supporters staged a series of disputations, or arguments, with Catholic officials. These disputes led to the foundation of the Swiss Reformed Church, which was founded on Zwingli's doctrines.

The Protestant Reformation had a major influence on Zürich. It led to the eradication of numerous Catholic customs, such as the selling of indulgences and the adoration of saints. It also led to the construction of a new educational system and a new social order.

The Protestant Reformation in Zürich was not without its problems. In 1531, Zwingli was murdered in combat against the Catholic cantons of Switzerland. However, his legacy went on, and the Swiss Reformed Church continued to develop and thrive.

Today, the Protestant Reformation is still an essential element of the history and culture of Zürich. The Grossmünster is a renowned tourist site, and it is still a focus of Protestant religion. The city also boasts several additional churches and museums that are related to the Reformation.

Here are some of the most notable personalities in the Protestant Reformation in Zürich:

1. Huldrych Zwingli: Zwingli was a clergyman at the Grossmünster who started to preach against the injustices of the Catholic Church in 1519. He was a compelling leader, and his views were popular with the people of Zürich. He was murdered in combat in 1531, yet his memory went on.

2. Heinrich Bullinger: Bullinger was Zwingli's successor as the head of the Swiss Reformed Church. He was a skilled theologian, and he helped to establish the church's teaching. He also published several notable publications on the Reformation.

3. Katharina von Zimmern: Von Zimmern was abbess of the Fraumünster, one of the most prominent churches in Zürich. She was a fervent supporter of the Reformation, and she worked to safeguard the church against Catholic onslaught. She was also a great writer, and she left behind a lot of noteworthy works.

The Protestant Reformation had a major influence on Zürich. It resulted in the foundation of the Swiss Reformed Church, which is still a prominent denomination in Switzerland today. It also led to the eradication of several Catholic customs, such as the selling of indulgences and the adoration of saints. The Reformation also had a considerable influence on the social and political order in Zürich.

The Protestant Reformation is still a significant element of the history and culture of Zürich today. The Grossmünster is a renowned tourist site, and it is still a focus of Protestant religion. The city also boasts several additional churches and museums that are related to the Reformation.

Disputations: The Grossmünster is home to a significant collection of works on the anniversary theme 'disputations'. These publications reflect the key theological arguments that took place during the Reformation.

Here are some interesting facts about the historic churches in Zürich:

1. The Grossmünster earned its name because it was constructed on the site of a Roman castrum, or fort. The term "münster" means "minster" or "cathedral" in German.

2. The bells of the Grossmünster were originally cooled with wet cow skins. This was done to keep them from breaking in the heat.

3. The interior of the Grossmünster was considerably different before the iconoclasm of the Reformation.

The walls were decorated with paintings and sculptures, much of which were destroyed during the iconoclastic uprisings.

4. Marc Chagall discovered glass painting while he was touring the Ste-Chapelle in Paris. He was so impressed by the stained glass windows there that he decided to become a glass painter himself.

5. The convent ladies of the Fraumünster were immensely strong in the Middle Ages. They had a vast amount of land and goods, and they even had an army.

6. The iconoclasm of the Reformation was a moment of considerable upheaval in Zürich. Many churches were demolished, and pieces of art were defaced. However, the Reformation also led to a blooming of new creative expression, as artists strove to develop new forms of religious art that were more in keeping with the Protestant faith.

7. Trams used to operate through the Münsterhof, the plaza in front of the Grossmünster. However, they were withdrawn in 1954.

8. There are a handful of women who played major roles in the Protestant Reformation. These include Huldrych Zwingli's wife, Anna Reinhard, and Katharina Zell, a German reformer who was famed for her fiery preaching.

There are a variety of guided excursions offered that examine the historic churches in Zürich. These tours are a terrific opportunity to learn about the history of the cathedrals and to view them in a more evocative context. Some of the guided tours include:

1. The Reformation trip: This trip covers the Grossmünster and the Fraumünster, and it highlights the tale of the Protestant Reformation in Zürich.

2. The Chagall Windows Tour: This tour concentrates on the iconic stained glass windows in the Fraumünster, and it relates the narrative of Marc Chagall's life and work.

3. The Night Tour: This tour takes place after dark, and it enables guests to explore the churches in a more evocative atmosphere.

1. Grossmünster (great minster)
Location: Zwinglipl. 7, 8001 Zürich, Switzerland
GPS Coordinate: 47.3697° N, 8.5414° E

Grossmünster was erected in the 12th century on the ruins of a Roman fort. It is a Romanesque-style church with two towers, which are visible from all across the city. The church was established by Charlemagne, and it was initially a monastic church. However, it was secularized in the 16th century during the Protestant Reformation. The church is dedicated to the Holy Forefathers, and its name means "Great Minster" in German.

There are a lot of tales and legends related to Grossmünster. One myth speaks of how the church was built by Charlemagne, who was claimed to have been inspired by a vision of the two towers. Another myth speaks of how the church was rescued from destruction during the Reformation by a group of ladies who concealed the keys to the church.

Grossmünster is intimately identified with the Swiss Reformation. It was here that Huldrych Zwingli, a key figure in the Reformation, gave his fiery sermons. The cathedral was also the location of the first public burning of the Catholic Mass book in 1523.

The architecture of Grossmünster is a blend of Romanesque and Gothic styles. The two towers are the most recognizable characteristics of the church.

They are 63 meters tall and they are capped with spires. The towers are composed of sandstone and they are ornamented with arcades and blind arcades.

The inside of Grossmünster is likewise quite remarkable. The nave is long and thin, and it is split into four bays. The ceiling is supported by pillars, and it is covered with paintings. The most renowned fresco in the cathedral is the Christ in Majesty, which is positioned in the apse.

The most notable feature of Grossmünster is the west rose window. This window is 10 meters in diameter, and it is made up of 100 separate pieces of stained glass. The window represents the Last Judgment, and it is one of the most significant pieces of art in Switzerland.

Grossmünster is home to a lot of noteworthy art and antiques. These include:

1. The Zwingli Monument: This monument was created in 1884 to memorialize Huldrych Zwingli.
2. The Leuthold Window: This window which is placed in the south transept, is the most renowned, and it was erected in 1520. It represents the martyrdom of Felix and Regula, the patron saints of Zürich.
3. The Bernoulli Organ: This organ was erected in 1733, and it is one of the most renowned organs in Switzerland.

Other famous artworks in Grossmünster include the Baptismal Font, which is made of marble, and the High Altar, which is built of wood. The chapel also holds several important manuscripts and books.

Grossmünster is available to the public for visits. Admission is free. The church is open from 07:00 to 18:00, Monday to Saturday, and from 09:00 to 17:00, Sunday. There are a variety of guided tours of Grossmünster that are offered.

These trips are given in several languages, including English, German, and French.

The church is situated in the Old Town of Zürich, and it is readily accessible by public transit. The closest tram station is named "Grossmünster."

In addition to Grossmünster, there are several other historical sites in the vicinity. These include the Fraumünster, the Lindenhof, and the Zürich City Hall. There are also a lot of restaurants and stores in the neighborhood, so you can easily find something to eat or do before or after your visit to Grossmünster.

2. Fraumünster
Location: Münsterhof 2, 8001 Zürich, Switzerland
GPS Coordinate: 47.3697° N, 8.5414° E

The Fraumünster was established in 853 by Louis the German for his daughter Hildegard. It was formerly a Benedictine monastery, but it was secularized in 1524 during the Protestant Reformation. The church was constructed in the 19th century, and it presently belongs to the Evangelical Reformed Church of the Canton of Zürich.

There are a lot of tales and legends related to the Fraumünster. One tradition speaks of how Hildegard, the first abbess of the monastery, was visited by an angel who urged her to erect a church on the location. Another myth speaks of how the church was rescued from destruction during the Protestant Reformation by a group of ladies who concealed the church's riches.

The Fraumünster is a Romanesque-Gothic church with a lovely cloister. The most prominent feature of the cathedral is the stained glass windows, which were created by Marc Chagall in the 1960s. The windows portray scenes from the Old and New Testaments, and they are some of the most renowned stained glass windows in the world.

The Fraumünster also includes a variety of other artworks, including paintings by Hans Holbein the Younger and a sculpture of Hildegard by Ferdinand Hodler. The cathedral also features a crypt that holds the bones of some of the past abbesses of the convent.

The Fraumünster is situated in the center of Zürich, only a short walk from the Grossmünster. It is available to the public from 10 am to 6 pm every day, and entrance is free. The Fraumünster is a famous tourist site, and it is regularly busy. If you want to escape the crowds, I suggest arriving early in the morning or late in the day. The church is also an excellent destination to visit if you are interested in art or architecture. There are also guided tours offered in German, English, French, and Italian.

I have visited Fraumünster several times, and I always like it. The stained glass windows are exceptionally stunning, and I always discover something new to enjoy each time I return. I appreciate the serene environment of the church, and I find it to be a fantastic place to rest and contemplate.
I hope you enjoy your visit to the Fraumünster!

3. Predigerkirche (Preacher's Church)
Location: Zahringer. 6, 8001 Zürich, Switzerland
GPS Coordinate: 47.3738° N, 8.5454° E

Predigerkirche was established in the 13th century by the Dominican Order, and it is one of the four principal churches in the Old Town of Zürich. It was initially a Romanesque church, but it was reconstructed in the Gothic style in the 14th century.

The cathedral was the location of several significant events in Swiss history, notably the marriage of Huldrych Zwingli and Anna Reinhard in 1522. Zwingli was a Protestant reformer who was influential in the foundation of the Swiss Reformed Church.

The cathedral is notable for its exquisite stained glass windows, which were constructed by some of the most prominent painters of the period, including Hans Holbein the Younger.

There are a variety of tales and legends related to Predigerkirche. One tale talks of a spirit that haunts the chapel. The ghost is claimed to be the spirit of a Dominican friar who was slain in the cathedral in the 15th century.

The Predigerkirche is a wonderful specimen of Gothic architecture. The church comprises a long nave, a choir, and a transept. The nave is supported by a series of pillars, and the choir is crowned by a lovely rose window. The church is composed of sandstone, and it is embellished with a variety of sculptures and carvings.

The Predigerkirche is home to a multitude of exquisite art and treasures. The most renowned of them is the Holbein Window, which was built by Hans Holbein the Younger in 1505. The window shows the Last Judgment, and it is regarded to be one of the most significant pieces of art in Switzerland. The church also has several additional stained glass windows, as well as sculptures, paintings, and tapestries, many of which were constructed in the 15th and 16th centuries.

The Predigerkirche is available to the public from 10:00 AM to 5:00 PM, every day of the week, except Mondays, which is noon. Admission is free. The church is situated in the Old Town of Zürich, near Grossmünster. You may reach there by taking the tram to the Central Station, or by walking from the Niederdorf.

If you're interested in knowing more about Predigerkirche, there is a museum housed in the church that holds a collection of objects and papers relating to the church's history. The museum is available to the public for a modest price.

I always find it to be a serene and inspirational area. I appreciate the magnificent architecture and the rich history of the church. I would strongly suggest seeing Predigerkirche if you're ever in Zürich

4. St. Peter's Church
Location: St. Peter Hofstatt 1, 8001 Zürich, Switzerland
GPS Coordinate: 47.3711° N, 8.5407° E

St. Peter's Church is situated in the middle of the Old Town, only a short walk from Grossmünster. It's the oldest parish church in Zürich, and its striking clock face is one of the most identifiable views in the city. The church is named for Saint Peter, one of the twelve apostles of Jesus Christ. Saint Peter is regarded to be the first pope, and he is the patron saint of Zürich. The church is readily accessible by public transit, and there are various restaurants and stores nearby.

St. Peter's Church was erected on the site of a Roman temple to Jupiter. The earliest church on the site was erected in the 9th century, but it was destroyed by fire in 1230. The present edifice was created in the 14th century, and it's a superb example of Gothic architecture.

The outside of the church is composed of sandstone, and it boasts a tall, thin tower. The tower is 51 meters tall, and it's the tallest clock face in Europe. The inside of the church is extremely remarkable. The nave is 100 meters long, and it's packed with stunning stained glass windows. The windows were produced by some of the most prominent painters of the Middle Ages, including Hans Holbein the Younger.

St. Peter's Church is a famous tourist site, and it's also a favorite venue for weddings and other special occasions. The church is accessible to the public every day, and there are guided tours available.

St. Peter's Church is home to numerous significant pieces of art, including a painting of the Last Supper by Hans Holbein the Younger. There are also various stained glass windows in the church, some of which were produced by notable artisans of the Middle Ages.

There are guided tours available, and the church also hosts a variety of special events throughout the year.

Opening time: Sundays, 11 am- 5 pm, Monday to Friday, 8 am- 6 pm, and Saturdays 10 am-4 pm

5. Wasserkirche (Water Church)
Location: Limmatquai 31, 8001 Zürich, Switzerland
GPS Coordinate: 47.3698° N, 8.5432° E

The Wasserkirche, or "Water Church," is a lovely church built on a tiny island in the Limmat River in Zürich, Switzerland. It is one of the oldest churches in the city, dating back to the 10th century. It is situated in the Old Town of Zürich, between the Grossmünster and Fraumünster churches. The church is available to the public from 9 a.m. to 5 p.m., and there is no entry fee.

The church was initially devoted to Saint Felix, but it was afterward dedicated to Saint Regula as well. It was initially erected in a place that was holy to the Celts, and according to stories, the two patron saints of Zürich, Felix, and Regula, were executed on this spot in the 3rd century. The church was renovated multiple times throughout the years, and it was eventually given its present Gothic style in the 15th century.

The Wasserkirche is a famous tourist site, and it is also a favorite location for residents to relax and enjoy the scenery. The church is available to the public, and there is no entry price.

The Wasserkirche is a wonderful specimen of Gothic architecture. The church features a long nave with a high vaulted roof.

The walls of the church are ornamented with stained glass windows. The most renowned stained glass window in the cathedral is the "Blue Madonna," which was produced in the 15th century. The church also features a crypt where the bones of Felix and Regula are reported to be interred.

The Wasserkirche is a favorite area for folks to relax and enjoy the scenery. The chapel is surrounded by a park, and there is a small café on the island. The church is also a popular venue for weddings and concerts. There is also a tradition that suggests that if you stand on the island at midnight and listen closely, you may hear the bells of the church ringing.

Contemporary Art and Theaters

1. The Kunsthaus Zürich

The Kunsthaus Zürich was created in 1898, and it is one of the biggest and most prominent museums of modern and contemporary art in Switzerland. The museum is situated in the center of Zürich, and it includes a collection of almost 40,000 pieces of art, including paintings, sculptures, drawings, prints, and photos. The Kunsthaus Zürich is home to a variety of iconic pieces of art, including Vincent van Gogh's Sunflowers, Pablo Picasso's Les Demoiselles d'Avignon, and Edvard Munch's The Scream. The museum has also held several noteworthy exhibits, including the first major retrospective of the work of Alberto Giacometti in 1955.

Architecture:
1. The Kunsthaus Zürich was created by the Swiss architect Karl Moser, and it is an example of Art Nouveau architecture.
2. The museum's front is ornamented with a variety of sculptures, including The Three Graces by Carl Burckhardt.
3. The interior of the museum is separated into several galleries, which are organized chronologically.

Contemporary Art:
1. The Kunsthaus Zürich has a large collection of contemporary art, and it often holds exhibits of new work by young and recognized artists.
2. The museum has also been at the forefront of collecting and exhibiting video art, and it was one of the first museums in the world to devote an entire gallery to the medium.
3. The Kunsthaus Zürich's collection of contemporary art includes works by artists such as Andy Warhol, Jeff Koons, and Damien Hirst.

Tourism Information:
Opening time: Tue, Fri – Sun 10 a.m. – 6 p.m. Wed – Thu 10 a.m. – 8 p.m. Closed on Mondays
GPS Coordinate: 47.3708° N, 8.5488° E
Phone: +41 44 253 84 84
Website: https://www.kunsthaus.ch/en/
Admission is CHF 25 for adults, CHF 15 for students and seniors, and free for children under 16.
Address: Heimplatz 1/5, 8001 Zürich, Switzerland.
The closest tram station is Kunsthaus, which is serviced by lines 2 and 4.
The Kunsthaus Zürich is a renowned tourist site, and it is typically busy during the high season.
The museum provides a variety of guided tours, which are a terrific opportunity to learn more about the collection.
The Kunsthaus Zürich also features a variety of educational programs for children and adults.

2. Migros Museum für Gegenwartskunst (The Migros Museum of Contemporary Art)
The Migros Museum für Gegenwartskunst was created in 1996 by the Migros Group, a Swiss retail and food cooperative. The museum is situated in the city of Zürich, and its collection concentrates on contemporary art from the 1960s to the present day.

The museum's building was created by the Swiss architectural company Gigon/Guyer. The structure is composed of concrete and glass, and it includes a remarkable spiral staircase.

Architecture:
The museum's architecture is a combination of contemporary and traditional features. The concrete outside is straightforward and plain, but the glass inside is light and spacious. The spiral staircase is a main aspect of the structure, and it gives visitors a unique vantage position from which to see the exhibits.

Contemporary Art:
The museum's collection contains works by a broad spectrum of contemporary artists, including Cindy Sherman, Jeff Koons, and Olafur Eliasson. The museum regularly offers temporary exhibits of modern art.

The museum's collection is always developing, and it is an excellent site to observe the current trends in contemporary art. The museum also provides a range of educational events, making it an excellent venue to learn about modern art.

Tourism Information:
The Migros Museum für Gegenwartskunst is situated at Limmatstrasse 270 in Zürich. The museum is open from Tuesday to Sunday, from 11 am to 6 pm. It is closed on Mondays and public holidays. Admission is CHF 20 for adults, CHF 15 for elderly and students, and free for children under 16.

The museum is accessible to individuals with impairments. There is a ramp going up to the entrance, and there are accessible facilities on the ground level. There is little parking accessible near the museum. There is a public parking garage available at Limmatquai 11, which is a short walk from the museum.

The museum is affiliated with the Migros Art Collection, which is one of the greatest private art collections in Switzerland. The museum has held several major exhibits, including "The Body in Question" (2002) and "The Art of the Sixties" (2006). The museum is situated in the center of Zürich, near other attractions such as the Kunsthaus Zürich and the Grossmünster.
Website: www.migrosmuseum.ch
Address: Limmatstrasse 270, 8005 Zürich, Switzerland
GPS Coordinate: 47.389389°N 8.524889°E
Phone: +41 44 277 20 50

3. The Schauspielhaus Zürich (Zürich theater)
The Schauspielhaus Zürich is one of the most notable and influential theaters in the German-speaking world. It is also known as "Pfauenbühne" (Peacock Stage). It was formed in 1892 by a group of performers and directors who were unsatisfied with the status of theater in Zürich at the time. The theater's debut presentation was a play by the Swiss dramatist Gottfried Keller. The theater immediately established a reputation for its high-quality presentations and its devotion to new and experimental work.

In 1901, the Schauspielhaus Zürich relocated into a new facility constructed by the Swiss architect Karl Moser. The building was created in the Art Nouveau style and features a striking red brick exterior. The theater's new venue enabled it to extend its repertoire and to recruit even more skilled performers and directors.

In the early 20th century, the Schauspielhaus Zürich became an important hub for the development of contemporary theater. The theater featured the première of several famous plays, including Bertolt Brecht's The Threepenny Opera in 1928. The theater also became recognized for its inventive shows, which frequently defied established norms.

During World War II, the Schauspielhaus Zürich was forced to shut down for a while. However, it reopened in 1945 and continued to create high-quality work. In the years after the war, the theater has featured several world-renowned performers and directors, including Max Reinhardt, Peter Brook, and Luc Bondy.

Today, the theater continues to perform a broad spectrum of modern plays, from classical classics to innovative experimental creations. The theater also organizes a variety of festivals and events, such as the Zürich Theater Spektakel.

The Schauspielhaus Zürich is an important cultural institution in Zürich and Switzerland as a whole. The theater has played a vital part in the creation of contemporary theater and continues to be a prominent force in the performing arts. The huge theater contains 750 seats. The Schauspielhaus Zürich is situated in the center of Zürich, near other attractions such as the Kunsthaus Zürich and the Grossmünster.

Here are some of the activities that they do in the Schauspielhaus Zürich:

1. Produce plays: The theater company creates a new season of plays every year, which comprises a mix of traditional pieces, new plays, and experimental shows.
2. Host festivals and events: The Schauspielhaus Zürich holds a variety of festivals and events throughout the year, such as the Zürich Theater Spektakel, which is a festival of contemporary theater and performance art.
3. Offer guided tours: The theater offers guided tours of the building, which give guests a chance to learn about the theater's history and architecture.
4. Run a bookstore: The theater has a bookshop that sells books on theater, as well as books by playwrights and directors who have worked at the theater.

5. **Offer seminars:** The theater offers a range of workshops for actors, directors, and other theatrical professionals.

Tourism Information:
The Schauspielhaus Zürich is situated in Rämistrasse 34 in Zürich. The theater is open from Tuesday through Sunday, from 11 a.m. to 6 p.m. Admission charges vary based on the performance. The Schauspielhaus Zürich provides a range of guided tours and courses. There is also a café and a bookstore on the site.
GPS Coordinate: 47.3702° N, 8.5492° E
Address: Rämistrasse 34, 8001 Zürich, Switzerland
Phone: +41 44 258 77 77
Seating capacity: 750
Website: https://www.schauspielhaus.ch/de/

4. Tanzhaus Zürich
The Tanzhaus Zürich was formed in 1996 by a group of dancers, choreographers, and producers who were unsatisfied with the condition of dance in Zürich at the time. The theater's inaugural show was a dance work by the Swiss choreographer Marco Canevacci. The theater immediately established a reputation for its high-quality presentations and its devotion to new and experimental work.

The Tanzhaus Zürich is situated in the old Wasserwerk building in Zürich-Wipkingen. The structure was initially erected in 1894 as a water treatment facility, but it was turned into a theater in 1996. The structure features a unique red brick front and a huge auditorium with a capacity of 240 seats.

In the early 2000s, the Tanzhaus Zürich became a prominent hub for the development of contemporary dance. The theater held the première of several major dance works, including Crowd by Anne Teresa De Keersmaeker in 2000 and Metamorphoses by Pina Bausch in 2001. The theater also became recognized for its inventive shows, which frequently defied established norms.

Today, the Tanzhaus Zürich is one of the most prominent dance theaters in the world. The theater continues to create a broad spectrum of modern dance performances, from traditional works to new experimental creations. The theater also organizes a variety of festivals and events, such as the Tanznacht Zürich, which is a night-long festival of dance.

The Tanzhaus Zürich is an important cultural institution in Zürich and Switzerland as a whole. The theater has played a vital influence in the creation of modern dance and continues to be a driving force in the performing arts.

The Tanzhaus Zürich's building was created by the Swiss architect Max Vogt in the Art Nouveau style. The structure features a unique red brick front and a huge auditorium with a capacity of 240 seats. The auditorium is flanked by a variety of smaller performing venues, including a black box theater and a rehearsal area.

The Tanzhaus Zürich does not maintain a permanent collection of contemporary art, although it does host several exhibits of contemporary dance and performance art. The theater also offers a bookstore that sells books on dance, as well as books by choreographers and dancers who have worked at the theater.

The Tanzhaus Zürich is situated at Wasserwerkstrasse 127a in Zurich. The theater is open from Tuesday through Sunday, from 11 a.m. to 6 p.m. Admission charges vary based on the performance. The Tanzhaus Zürich provides a range of guided tours and courses. There is also a café and a bookstore on the site.

Other Information:
The Tanzhaus Zürich is affiliated with the Tanzhaus Zürich Stiftung, a private organization that supports the theater.

The theater has held several major debuts, including the first performance of Crowd by Anne Teresa De Keersmaeker in 2000 and Metamorphoses by Pina Bausch in 2001.
The Tanzhaus Zürich is situated in the center of Zürich, adjacent to other attractions such as the Kunsthaus Zürich and the Grossmünster.
Address: Wasserwerkstrasse 127a, 8037 Zürich, Switzerland
Phone: +41 44 350 26 10
GPS Coordinate: 47.3702° N, 8.5492° E
Website: https://www.tanzhaus-zuerich.ch/en/

5. Museum of Design Zürich (Museum für Gestaltung Zürich)
The Museum of Design Zürich was created in 1880 as the Schweizerisches Landesmuseum für Industrie und Arbeit (Swiss National Museum for Industry and Labor). The museum was renamed in 2007 to highlight its emphasis on design.

The museum's initial location was a disused cotton mill in Zürich-Enge. The museum relocated to its present home in 1956, a former industrial building in Zürich-West. The structure was created by the Swiss architect Max Frisch.

The museum has a long and colorful history. It has been host to several major exhibits, including the first exhibition of Bauhaus design in Switzerland in 1931. The museum has also played a key influence in the development of Swiss design.

The museum has been host to several major exhibits, including the first exhibition of Bauhaus design in Switzerland in 1931. The museum has also played a key influence in the development of Swiss design.

Here are some of the highlights of the museum's extensive history:

1880: The museum was formed as the Schweizerisches Landesmuseum für Industrie und Arbeit (Swiss National Museum for Industry and Labor).
1931: The museum holds the first exhibition of Bauhaus design in Switzerland.
1956: The museum moves to its present home in Zürich-West.
1970: The museum unveils a new wing devoted to the history of graphic design.
1996: The museum unveils a new wing devoted to the history of product design.
2007: The institution is renamed the institution für Gestaltung Zürich (Museum of Design Zürich).
2014: The museum unveils a new section devoted to the history of fashion.

Architecture:
The Museum of Design Zürich is housed in a former industrial building in Zürich-West. The building was created by the Swiss architect Max Frisch in the International Style. The building features a unique red brick front and a big glass-and-steel entry hall.

Contemporary Art:
The Museum of Design Zürich showcases a broad spectrum of design artifacts, from furniture and fashion to product design and graphic design. The museum also has a major emphasis on current design.

Tourism Information:
The Museum of Design Zürich is situated at Seefeldstrasse 101 in Zürich. The museum is open from Tuesday to Sunday, from 11 am to 6 pm. Admission is CHF 15 for adults.

Additional Information:
The museum provides a range of educational events, such as workshops and seminars. There is also a store on the site.

The Museum of Design Zürich is an important cultural institution in Zürich and in Switzerland as a whole. The museum is devoted to examining the history and practice of design, and it plays an essential role in showcasing Swiss design to a worldwide audience.

What do they do there?
The Museum of Design Zürich provides a range of activities and events, including:

1. Permanent exhibits: The museum contains a variety of permanent displays, which reflect the history of design from the Industrial Revolution to the current day.
2. Temporary exhibits: The museum holds a variety of temporary exhibitions each year, which concentrate on certain themes of design.
3. Educational activities: The museum provides a range of educational programs, such as seminars, lectures, and tours.
4. Events: The museum conducts a variety of events each year, such as design discussions, film screenings, and concerts.
Website: https://museum-gestaltung.ch/en/
GPS Coordinates:
Pfingstweidstrasse 96 8005 Zürich: 47.377011 N, 8.539775 E
Ausstellungsstrasse 60 8005 Zürich: 47.376814° N, 8.539826° E
Address: The Museum of Design Zürich has two locations:
1. Main location: The main location is situated at Ausstellungsstrasse 60 8005 Zürich. This is the biggest of the two venues and it is home to the museum's permanent displays, as well as temporary exhibitions, educational activities, and events.
2. Plakatraum: The Plakatraum is situated at Pfingstweidstrasse 96 8005 Zürich. This is a minor site that is devoted to the history of Swiss posters.

Opening hours: Tuesday–Sunday 10 am–5 pm, Thursday 10 am–8 pm, Monday closed

6. Landesmuseum Zürich (Swiss National Museum)

The Landesmuseum Zürich (Swiss National Museum) was created in 1898 by the Swiss federal government. The museum is situated in the center of Zürich, on the beaches of Lake Zürich. The notion of a Swiss National Museum was initially mooted in the 1870s. The Swiss federal government was interested in constructing a museum that would display the country's cultural history.

In 1891, the Swiss government organized a competition to design the museum. The winning design was presented by the Swiss architect Gustav Gull. Gull's design was influenced by the Neo-Renaissance style, which was prominent at the time.

The museum's initial structure was erected in 1902. The structure was opened on June 25, 1902, with a magnificent ceremony. The inaugural show at the museum was the first display of Swiss archaeology.

The Landesmuseum Zürich has undergone a lot of modifications and extensions throughout the years. The most recent refurbishment was conducted in 2008. The refurbishment involved the creation of a new display hall, as well as the restoration of the museum's original Neo-Renaissance characteristics.

Here are some of the highlights of the museum's history:

1891: The Swiss government launched a competition to design the Swiss National Museum.
1902: The museum's initial building is finished.
1903: The first exhibition of Swiss archaeology is presented at the museum.

1931: The museum holds the first exhibition of Bauhaus design in Switzerland.
1952: The museum is extended to incorporate a new wing devoted to Swiss history.
1991: The museum commemorates its 100th anniversary.
2008: The museum receives a substantial refurbishment.

Architecture:
The Landesmuseum Zürich is a massive Neo-Renaissance edifice with a unique red brick front. The structure features a central courtyard and it is encircled by a variety of display spaces.

Contemporary Art:
The Landesmuseum Zürich showcases a broad variety of antiquities, from ancient artifacts to current art. The museum also has a major emphasis on Swiss history and culture.

Tourism Information:
The Landesmuseum Zürich is situated at Museumstrasse 2 in Zürich. The museum is open from Tuesday through Sunday, from 10 am to 5 pm. Admission is CHF 15 for adults.

Additional Information:
The museum provides a range of educational events, such as workshops and seminars. There is also a store on the site.

What do they do there?
The Landesmuseum Zürich provides a range of activities and events, including:

1. Permanent exhibits: The museum features a variety of permanent displays, which reflect the history of Switzerland from the Stone Age to the current day.
2. Temporary exhibits: The museum holds a variety of temporary exhibitions each year, which concentrate on certain elements of Swiss history and culture.

3. **Educational activities:** The museum provides a range of educational programs, such as seminars, lectures, and tours.
4. **Events:** The museum conducts a variety of events each year, including concerts, festivals, and discussions.
Address: Museumstrasse 2, 8001 Zürich, Switzerland
Opening hours: Tuesdays to Sundays, 10.00 AM - 5.00 PM. They closed on Mondays
Phone: +41 44 218 65 11
GPS Coordinate: 47.3791° N, 8.5405° E
Tickets: https://tickets.landesmuseum.ch/en
Website: https://www.landesmuseum.ch/en

Architectural Marvels & Historical Buildings

1. Viadukt
We're going to be touring the Viadukt, a former railway viaduct that has been turned into a pedestrian and cycling bridge. It's a popular site for residents and visitors alike, and it's a terrific area to roam about and explore.

The Viadukt was constructed in the 1890s to bring trains from the city center to the outskirts. However, the trains ceased operating in the 1980s, and the viaduct was abandoned. In the early 2000s, the city of Zürich planned to transform the viaduct into a pedestrian and cycling bridge. The renovation was finished in 2004, and the Viadukt was opened to the public.

The Viadukt is currently home to a multitude of stores, restaurants, and pubs. There's also a farmers market that takes place on the bridge every Saturday. The Viadukt is a fantastic spot to meander about and do some shopping or people-watching. You may also eat a meal at one of the restaurants, or simply take a pause and appreciate the views.

If you're searching for a unique and intriguing site to visit in Zürich, I strongly suggest the Viadukt.

It's a terrific spot to spend a day, and it's guaranteed to leave you with some amazing memories.

Here are some extra things that first-time visitors to the Viadukt should know:
- The Viadukt is situated in the neighborhood of Zürich West.
- The bridge is open 24 hours a day, 7 days a week.
- There is no entry cost to see the Viadukt.
- There are a lot of parking garages available near the Viadukt.
- The Viadukt is a popular attraction for both residents and visitors, so it may become busy, particularly on weekends.

2. Zürich Opera House
If you're a first-timer in Zürich, I strongly suggest seeing the Zürich Opera House. It's one of the most beautiful and recognizable structures in the city, and it's host to some of the top opera and ballet performances in the world.

The Zürich Opera House was erected in the 1890s, and it's a gem of Art Nouveau architecture. The front of the structure is covered with exquisite sculptures and mosaics, and the inside is just as gorgeous. The auditorium is a huge hall with a crimson velvet roof and gold leaf decorations.

The Zürich Opera Company is one of the most significant opera companies in the world. They present a broad variety of operas, from classic works to new commissions. The firm also boasts a world-renowned ballet troupe.

If you're interested in witnessing a performance at the Zürich Opera House, I suggest buying your tickets well in advance. The opera house is quite popular, and tickets often sell out rapidly.

Here are some additional things to know about the Zürich Opera House:
- The opera building is situated on Falkenstrasse, on the beaches of Lake Zürich.
- The opera house is open from Monday through Saturday, from 10 am to 5 pm.
- Admission to the opera house is CHF 20 for adults.
- There are a lot of guided tours of the opera theater available.
- The opera building is also home to a variety of restaurants and pubs.

3. Lindenhof

Lindenhof is a hill in the center of the city that gives panoramic views of Zürich and the surrounding region. It's a terrific spot to relax and take in the scenery, and it's also home to a variety of historical sites, including the remnants of a Roman fort.

The hill was initially occupied by the Romans in the 1st century AD. They erected a fort atop the hill to safeguard their village against the Germanic tribes. The fort was subsequently abandoned, although the remnants may still be seen today.

In the Middle Ages, Lindenhof was the location of several major events. In 1298, the Swiss beat the Austrians in the Battle of Morgarten, which is regarded to be one of the most significant engagements in Swiss history. The fight was fought on the hills of Lindenhof, and the Swiss victory helped to win their independence from Austria.

In the 18th century, Lindenhof became a favorite site for painters and authors. The poet Gottfried Keller resided on the hill for a while, and he wrote about it in his poem "Lindenhof."

Today, Lindenhof is a renowned tourist site. It's a nice area to rest and take in the views, and it's also a terrific place to learn about the history of Zürich.

Here are some activities you can do on Lindenhof:
1. Visit the remains of the Roman fort: The remnants of the Roman fort are positioned on the summit of the hill. They're a short walk from the main entrance of Lindenhof.
2. Enjoy the panoramic vistas: The views from Lindenhof are magnificent. You can view all of Zürich and the surrounding region.
3. Learn about the history of Zürich: Several information boards on Lindenhof describe the tale of the hill's history.
4. Relax at the park: There's a park on Lindenhof where you can relax and enjoy the surroundings.
5. Have a picnic: There are a lot of picnic tables on Lindenhof where you can have a picnic.

CHAPTER EIGHT

SHOPPING IN ZÜRICH

Welcome to Chapter 8 of our travel guide to Zürich, where we'll be examining the greatest locations to shop in the city. Whether you're searching for upscale stores and designer labels, or local markets and unique souvenirs, Zürich offers something for everyone.

In this chapter, we'll be visiting some of the most prominent retail areas in Zürich, including Bahnhofstrasse, Niederdorf, and the Old Town. We'll also be checking out some of the city's greatest local markets, where you can get anything from fresh food to handcrafted handicrafts.

So whether you're a serious shopper or simply seeking to browse, I'm confident you'll find something to your satisfaction in Zürich. Let's get started!

Renowned Shopping Districts

Here are some of the notable retail areas in Zürich:

1. Bahnhofstrasse: Bahnhofstrasse is the most renowned retail street in Zürich. It's home to a broad assortment of luxury stores and designer labels, including Prada, Gucci, and Louis Vuitton.

2. Niederdorf: Niederdorf is a pedestrianized neighborhood in the Old Town that's noted for its fashionable stores, art galleries, and restaurants.

3. Theaterstrasse: Theaterstrasse is a small street that runs parallel to Bahnhofstrasse. It's home to a variety of high-end fashion businesses, as well as some more inexpensive selections.

4. Brunnengasse: Brunnengasse is a short lane in the Old Town that's dotted with stores offering anything from souvenirs to antiques.

5. Schipfe: Schiffe is a quayside district that's home to a variety of retailers, galleries, and cafés. It's a nice spot to roam around and investigate.

6. Modacity: Modacity is a fashion and lifestyle concept shop that's situated in the Old Town. It's a terrific location to uncover unique and independent companies.

7. Hardstrasse: Hardstrasse is a street in the district of Zürich-West that's recognized for its independent boutiques and vintage businesses.

8. Limmatquai: Limmatquai is a quayside promenade that's dotted with stores, cafés, and restaurants. It's a fantastic spot to wander down and do some window shopping.

9. Viadukt: Viadukt is a disused railway viadukt that's been turned into a retail arcade. It's home to a lot of independent stores, as well as a food market.

10. Manufactum: Manufactum is a department store that's recognized for its high-quality, sustainable merchandise. It's a terrific location to purchase presents and souvenirs that are meant to last.

These are just a handful of the numerous prominent retail areas in Zürich. There are many other fantastic locations to shop in the city, so be sure to explore and pick your favorites.

Luxury Boutiques and Designer Brands

1. Bulgari
Bulgari Zürich GPS Coordinate: 47.3715° N, 8.5384° E
Address: Bahnhofstrasse 25, 8001 Zürich, Switzerland
Phone: +41 43 330 31 00
Website: Bulgari
https://www.bulgari.com/en-us/storelocator/country-region/switzerland/zh/Zürich/bahnhofstrasse-25
Opening Hours: 10 am - 6pm (Mondays through Saturdays), closed on Sundays.

This Italian jeweler has been in business since 1884 and is noted for its magnificent items. It is a premium jewelry and watches business situated at Bahnhofstrasse 25, one of the most exclusive shopping districts in the world. The shop is within walking distance of several other renowned tourist locations, such as the Grossmünster Cathedral and the Kunsthaus art gallery.

The shop is set in a stunning Art Deco building and showcases a large assortment of Bulgari's distinctive items, including Serpenti jewelry, B.zero1 watches, and Divas' Dream rings. These items are all famous designs that are guaranteed to turn attention.

Here are some of the items you may discover at Bulgari Zürich:

1. Jewelry: Bulgari is recognized for its magnificent jewelry, which is typically inspired by nature and mythology. Some of their most popular items are the Serpenti necklace, the B.zero1 ring, and the Divas' Dream bracelet.

2. Timepieces: Bulgari also creates high-end timepieces, which are noted for their opulent design and exquisite workmanship. Some of their most popular timepieces are the Octo Finissimo, the Serpenti Tubogas, and the Diagono.

3. Accessories: In addition to jewelry and watches, Bulgari also offers a range of luxury accessories, such as purses, sunglasses, and perfumes.

If you are searching for a genuinely premium shopping experience, then Bulgari Zürich is the right location to come. The boutique is home to some of the most exquisite and rare jewelry and timepieces in the world, and the staff are professionals in helping you discover the appropriate item for your requirements.

Prices: Bulgari is a premium brand, thus its items come with a hefty price tag. However, the quality of the jewelry and timepieces is top-notch, and they make a terrific keepsake or present for a loved one.

Unique services: The Bulgari shop provides several unique services for its clients, such as engraving, gift wrapping, and financing. They also offer a staff of professionals who can assist you in finding the appropriate piece of jewelry or watch for your requirements.

2. Chanel
Chanel Zürich GPS Coordinate: 47.3715° N, 8.5384° E
Address: Bahnhofstrasse 39, 8001 Zürich, Switzerland
Phone: +41 43 330 31 00
Opening Hours: 10 am – 7 pm (Mondays to Saturdays)

This French design brand is recognized for its high-end apparel, accessories, and perfumes. It is a premium fashion company with a store situated at Bahnhofstrasse 39, one of the most exclusive shopping districts in the world. The shop is within walking distance of several other renowned tourist locations, such as the Grossmünster Cathedral and the Kunsthaus art gallery.

The shop is set in a stunning Art Deco building and showcases a large assortment of Chanel's distinctive products, including handbags, clothes, jewelry, and watches.

The boutique is open from 10 am to 7 pm Monday to Saturday, (they shut at 2 pm on Saturdays), and are closed on Sunday. You may reach them at +41 43 330 31 00.

Here are some of the items you may discover at Chanel Zürich:

1. Handbags: Chanel is recognized for its classic handbags, such as the 2.55 and the Boy Chanel. These bags are manufactured from high-quality fabrics and are typically embellished with the Chanel insignia.

2. Apparel: Chanel also produces a broad variety of apparel, including dresses, suits, and accessories. The outfit is noted for its classic and timeless look.

3. Jewelry: Chanel's jewelry line comprises necklaces, bracelets, earrings, and rings. The jewelry is generally created from gold, diamonds, and other expensive stones.

4. Timepieces: Chanel also creates high-end timepieces, which are noted for their exquisite design and excellent manufacturing. Some of their most popular timepieces are the J12 and the Première.

If you are searching for a genuinely premium shopping experience, then Chanel Zürich is the right location to come. The boutique is home to some of the most exquisite and rare fashion goods in the world, and the staff are professionals in helping you discover the appropriate piece for your requirements.

Unique services: The Chanel shop provides several unique services for its clients, such as engraving, gift wrapping, and financing. They also offer a staff of professionals that can assist you in finding the appropriate item of fashion for your requirements.

Overall, the Chanel store in Zürich is a terrific destination for people searching for a premium shopping experience. The employees are courteous and knowledgeable, and the items are top-notch. If you're searching for a distinctive item of fashion to recall your journey, make sure to check out Chanel.

3. Cartier Zürich
GPS Coordinate: 47.3721° N, 8.5381° E
Address: Bahnhofstrasse 47, 8001 Zürich, Switzerland
Phone: +41 44 211 11 41
Website: https://www.cartier.com/de-ch/
Opening Hours: Mondays through Saturdays (10 am -7 pm). Closed on Sundays.

This French jeweler is another legendary name that's been around for generations. It is a premium jewelry and watchmaking store situated at Bahnhofstrasse 47, one of the most elite shopping districts in the world. The shop is set in a stunning Art Deco building and showcases a large assortment of Cartier's trademark products, including jewelry, watches, and accessories.

The boutique is open from 10 am to 7 pm Monday to Saturday and closes on Sunday. You may reach them at +41 44 211 11 41

Here are some of the items you may discover at Cartier Zürich:
1. Jewelry: Cartier is recognized for its magnificent jewelry, which is typically inspired by nature and mythology. Some of their most popular items are the Love bracelet, the Trinity ring, and the Panthère necklace.

2. Timepieces: Cartier also creates high-end timepieces, which are noted for their beautiful design and exquisite manufacturing. Some of their most popular timepieces are the Tank, the Santos, and the Pasha.

3. Accessories: In addition to jewelry and watches, Cartier also offers a range of luxury accessories, such as purses, sunglasses, and perfumes.

If you are searching for a genuinely premium shopping experience, then Cartier Zürich is the right location to come. The boutique is home to some of the most exquisite and rare jewelry and timepieces in the world, and the staff are professionals in helping you discover the appropriate item for your requirements.

Prices: Cartier is a premium brand, thus its items come with a hefty price tag. However, the quality of the jewelry and timepieces is top-notch, and they make a terrific keepsake or present for a loved one.

Unique services: The Cartier shop provides several unique services for its clients, such as engraving, gift wrapping, and financing. They also offer a staff of professionals who can assist you in finding the appropriate piece of jewelry or watch for your requirements.

Overall, the Cartier store in Zürich is a terrific destination for people searching for a premium shopping experience. The employees are courteous and knowledgeable, and the items are top-notch. If you're searching for a particular piece of jewelry or watch to remember your journey, be sure to check out Cartier.

4. Hermès
Hermès Zürich GPS Coordinate: 47.3702° N, 8.5396° E
Address: Bahnhofstrasse 47, 8001 Zürich, Switzerland
Phone: +41 44 211 41 71
Website: https://www.cartier.com/de-ch/

Opening Hours: Mondays through Saturdays (10 am -7 pm). Closed on Sundays.

This French design brand is recognized for its premium leather products, scarves, and watches. It is a premium fashion company with a store situated at Bahnhofstrasse 31, one of the most exclusive shopping districts in the world. The shop is set in a stunning Art Deco structure and provides a large assortment of Hermès's distinctive products, including purses, scarves, ties, accessories, and home goods.

Here are some of the items you may discover at Hermès Zürich:

1. Handbags: Hermès is recognized for its classic handbags, such as the Kelly bag and the Birkin bag. These bags are manufactured from high-quality leather and are typically decorated with the Hermès emblem.

2. Scarves: Hermès scarves are crafted from the finest silk and are typically patterned with elaborate motifs. They are a popular option for presents and are also a terrific way to add a touch of elegance to your clothing.

3. Ties: Hermès ties are manufactured from the finest silk and are typically woven with elaborate designs. They are a popular option for males and are also a terrific way to add a touch of elegance to your wardrobe.

4. Accessories: Hermès also offers a range of accessories, including belts, wallets, and jewelry. These accessories are crafted from high-quality materials and are likely to endure for many years.

5. Home products: Hermès also offers a range of home goods, such as furniture, dinnerware, and fragrances.

These home items are manufactured from the best materials and are guaranteed to give a sense of elegance to your house.

The boutique is home to some of the most exquisite and rare fashion goods in the world, and the staff are professionals in helping you discover the appropriate piece for your requirements.

Here are some other facts that guests on a holiday in Zürich would want to know about the Hermès store:

Prices: Hermès is a premium brand, thus its items come with a hefty price tag. However, the quality of the fashion products is top-notch, and they make a terrific keepsake or present for a loved one.

Unique services: The Hermès shop provides several unique services for its clients, such as engraving, gift wrapping, and financing. They also offer a staff of professionals that can assist you in finding the appropriate item of fashion for your requirements.

The employees are courteous and knowledgeable, and the items are top-notch. If you're searching for a distinctive item of fashion to celebrate your visit, make sure to check out Hermès.

5. Louis Vuitton
Louis Vuitton Zürich GPS Coordinate: 47.3706° N, 8.5392° E
Address: Bahnhofstrasse 30, 8001 Zürich, Switzerland, & GLOBUS, Schweizergasse 11 8001 Zürich, Switzerland
Phone: +41 44 221 11 00
Opening Hours: Mondays to Fridays (10 am -7 pm), Saturdays (9:30 am - 6 pm). Closed on Sundays.

This French design brand is recognized for its unique monogrammed bags and luggage. There are 2 Louis Vuitton boutiques in Zürich, Switzerland.

Both locations provide a large assortment of Louis Vuitton items, including handbags, luggage, wallets, shoes, accessories, and more. They also provide customizing options, such as hot stamping and engraving.

The pricing of Louis Vuitton items in Zürich is comparable to the prices in other major cities in Europe. However, if you are a non-EU resident, you may claim a VAT refund after you leave Switzerland. This may save you a large amount of money. You may also save money by buying them at the Louis Vuitton shop in FoxTown, which is situated around 40 minutes from Zürich.

6. Prada
Prada Zürich GPS Coordinate: 47.3718° N, 8.5388° E
Address: Bahnhofstrasse 42, 8001 Zürich, Switzerland
Phone: +41 91 986 64 00
Opening hours: 10 am to 7 pm, Monday to Saturday
Website: https://www.prada.com/ww/en/store-locator/store.Zürich

This Italian fashion business is recognized for its clean and refined designs. The Prada store in Zürich is situated in the center of the city's retail area, on Bahnhofstrasse, which is recognized as the "most expensive shopping street in the world." The business is set in a stunning Art Nouveau structure that was originally erected in 1904. The structure has been painstakingly repaired and preserves its original characteristics, such as the stained glass windows and the marble staircase.

The Prada shop in Zürich is set across two stories. The bottom story is devoted to women's ready-to-wear, while the second floor holds the accessories, footwear, and perfume lines. The shop also provides a modest range of menswear.

The Prada shop in Zürich is designed in the brand's characteristic minimalist style. The walls are painted white, and the furniture is built of sleek, contemporary materials. The lighting is gentle and diffused, producing a warm and welcoming ambiance.

The workers at the Prada shop in Zürich are knowledgeable and friendly. They are pleased to help you in selecting the appropriate item for your requirements.

Here are some of the goods that you can discover in the Prada shop in Zürich:

1. **Women's ready-to-wear:** dresses, skirts, trousers, jackets, blouses, sweaters, coats
2. **Accessories:** purses, wallets, shoes, belts, sunglasses, jewelry
3. **Footwear:** sneakers, boots, sandals, heels
4. **Fragrances:** Men's and women's fragrances
5. **Cosmetics:** Makeup, skincare, and perfumes

If you are seeking high-quality, trendy, and luxury items, then the Prada store in Zürich is one of the best location for you to shop. The business is situated in a handy location and the staff is pleasant and educated.

7. Gucci
Gucci Zürich GPS Coordinate: 47.3716° N, 8.5383° E
Address: Bahnhofstrasse 39, 8001 Zürich, Switzerland
Phone: +41 44 211 46 20
Opening hours: 10 am to 7 pm, Monday to Saturday, closed on Sundays
Website: https://www.gucci.com/ch/de/store/bahnhofstrasse-39

The business is set in a stunning Art Deco structure that was initially erected in 1912. The structure has been painstakingly repaired and keeps its original characteristics, such as the terrazzo flooring and the Art Deco chandeliers.

The Gucci shop in Zürich is stretched across two stories. The ground floor is devoted to women's ready-to-wear, accessories, and footwear, while the second floor offers the men's range. The shop also includes a modest assortment of perfumes and cosmetics.

The Gucci shop in Zürich is adorned in the brand's characteristic maximalist manner. The walls are covered in vibrant designs, while the furniture is composed of expensive materials, such as marble and leather. The lighting is striking and provides a feeling of elegance.

The workers at the Gucci shop in Zürich are knowledgeable and friendly. They are pleased to help you in selecting the appropriate item for your requirements.

Here are some of the things that you may discover at the Gucci shop in Zürich:

1. Women's ready-to-wear: dresses, skirts, trousers, jackets, blouses, sweaters, coats
2. Accessories: purses, wallets, shoes, belts, sunglasses, jewelry
3. Footwear: sneakers, boots, sandals, heels
4. Men's ready-to-wear: suits, shirts, trousers, jackets, shoes, accessories
5. Fragrances: Men's and women's fragrances
6. Cosmetics: Makeup, skincare, and perfumes

In addition to the shop on Bahnhofstrasse, there is also a Gucci store in Zürich Airport. The airport shop is smaller than the one on Bahnhofstrasse, yet it nevertheless provides a broad assortment of Gucci items.

8. Dior
Dior Zürich GPS Coordinate: 47.3689° N, 8.5393° E
Phone: +41 44 215 68 80

Opening hours: 10 am to 7 pm, Monday to Saturday, closed on Sundays
Website: https://www.dior.com/fashion/stores/en_ch/switzerland/Zürich/bahnhofstrasse-13
Address: Bahnhofstrasse 13, 8001 Zürich, Switzerland
The business is set in a stunning Art Deco structure that was originally erected in 1928. The structure has been painstakingly repaired and keeps its original characteristics, such as the terrazzo flooring and the Art Deco chandeliers.

The Dior shop in Zürich is extended across two levels. The bottom story is devoted to women's ready-to-wear, while the second floor holds the accessories, footwear, and perfume lines. The shop also provides a modest range of menswear.

The Dior shop in Zürich is adorned in the brand's characteristic Art Deco style. The walls are painted white, while the furniture is constructed of dark wood and marble. The lighting is subtle and beautiful, providing a sumptuous ambiance.

The workers at the Dior shop in Zürich are informed and friendly. They are pleased to help you in selecting the appropriate item for your requirements.

Modes of Payment
These luxury boutiques in Zürich accept the following means of payment:
- Cash
- Credit cards (Visa, Mastercard, American Express, Diners Club)
- Debit cards
- Apple Pay
- Google Pay

They also provide financing alternatives for qualifying goods.

If you are paying with cash, you will need to pay in Swiss Francs. If you are paying with a credit card, debit card, or mobile payment, you may use your native currency or Swiss Francs. The businesses do not take personal checks or traveler's checks.

Here are some extra recommendations for paying at the luxury boutiques in Zürich:

1. If you are paying with a credit card, make sure to have your passport with you. The business may want to see your passport for identification reasons.
2. If you are paying using a debit card, make sure that your card has been enabled for foreign payments.
3. If you are paying with a mobile payment, make sure that your phone is unlocked and that you have a sufficient internet connection.
4. If you are paying with cash, make sure you have the precise amount of change. The shop does not offer change.

Local Markets and Unique Souvenirs

1. Rosenhof Market
Phone: +41 79 810 23 70
Website: https://rosenhof-markt.ch/
GPS Coordinate: 47.3729° N, 8.5433° E
Location: Rosenhof Market is situated in the Rosenhof, a lovely courtyard in the Old Town of Zürich. The actual location is Weingasse, 8001 Zürich, Switzerland.
Opening hours: The market is open every Thursday & Saturday from March to October, from 10:00 am to 6:00 pm.
What to expect: At Rosenhof Market, you'll discover a broad selection of vendors selling everything from local crafts and food to antiques and souvenirs. You may discover handcrafted jewelry, apparel, and accessories, as well as fresh fruit, flowers, and baked foods.

There are also a few food booths where you may enjoy typical Swiss delicacies, such as Zürcher Geschnetzeltes (a veal stew) and Rösti (a hash brown).

How to get there:
- **By public transportation:** The nearest tram station is Weingasse, which is serviced by trams 4 and 13.
- **By transport:** The nearest bus stop is Rosenhof, which is serviced by routes 62 and 63.
- **By foot:** The market is situated in the Old Town, therefore it is readily accessible by foot.
-

If you're traveling from outside of Zürich, you may take the train to Zürich Hauptbahnhof. From there, it's a short walk to the market.

Here are the steps to get to Rosenhof Market by car:
- Start by driving to Zürich.
- Once you're in Zürich, follow the signs towards the Old Town.
- Once you're in the Old Town, look for signs for Weingasse or Rosenhof.
- Park your vehicle at one of the parking facilities in the vicinity.
- Walk to the market, which is situated on Weingasse.

Tips:
1. If you're searching for souvenirs, be careful to barter with the sellers. They're typically ready to offer you a decent bargain.
2. If you're hungry, make sure to eat some of the classic Swiss cuisine at one of the food vendors.
3. If you're on a budget, make sure to visit the market on a Thursday. The prices are normally cheaper on Thursdays than on Saturdays.

2. Bürkliplatz Flea Market
GPS Coordinate: 47.367°N 8.541°E
This market is a hotspot for antique aficionados, collectors, and people interested in strange findings. The vendors, many of whom are specialists in their profession, congregate around Bahnhofstrasse, Fraumünsterstrasse, and the inner half of Bürkliplatz Square (Stadthausanlage).

Location: Bürkliplatz Flea Market is situated in **Bürkliplatz, 8001 Zürich, Switzerland.** It is positioned directly on the beaches of Lake Zürich and provides beautiful views of the city skyline. The market is also within walking distance of several other renowned tourist destinations, such as the Kunsthaus Zürich and the Swiss Federal Institute of Technology.

Opening hours: The market is open every Saturday from 7:00 a.m. to 5:00 p.m. from the 6th of May to the 28th of October. However, it is advisable to come early, since the greatest products tend to disappear fast. On weekdays, it is a standard food, vegetable, and fruit market.

What to expect: At Bürkliplatz Flea Market, you'll discover a broad selection of booths selling everything from antiques and collectibles to vintage clothes and furniture. You may also find food kiosks, as well as a few stalls offering souvenirs and presents. Here are some of the products you may find in the market:

- **Antiques:** Clocks, jewelry, furniture, toys, and other artifacts from the past
- **Collectibles:** Stamps, coins, baseball cards, and other artifacts that are collected by individuals
- **Vintage apparel:** Gowns, suits, caps, and other items from the past
- **Furniture:** Tables, chairs, couches, and other furniture from the past
- **Food:** sausages, pretzels, waffles, and other street food
- **Souvenirs:** Swiss chocolate, timepieces, and other products that signify Switzerland

How to get there:
- **By public transportation:** The nearest tram station is Bürkliplatz, which is serviced by trams 2, 4, 8, 11, and 15.
- **By water:** The market is also accessible by boat. The nearest boat port is Bürkliplatz, which is handled by the Zürichsee Schifffahrtsgesellschaft.

If you're traveling from outside of Zürich, you may take the train to Zürich Hauptbahnhof. From there, it's a short walk to the market.

Here are the instructions on how to arrive at Bürkliplatz Flea Market via car:
- Start by driving to the Zürich Hauptbahnhof.
- Once you're at the Hauptbahnhof, take the Sihlquai exit.
- Follow the signs towards Bürkliplatz.
- Once you approach Bürkliplatz, you'll notice the flea market on your left.
-

Here are the instructions on how to go to Bürkliplatz Flea Market via public transportation:
- Take the tram to Bürkliplatz.
- Once you get off the tram, stroll to the left and you'll find the flea market.

Tips:
- **Try to negotiate with the sellers.** They're typically ready to offer you a decent bargain.
- **If you're shopping for certain things, make sure to come early.** The better goods tend to go fast.
- **If you're hungry, make sure to eat some of the cuisine at one of the food vendors.** There are a range of alternatives to pick from, including traditional Swiss gastronomy and foreign cuisine.

- **Bring sunscreen and a hat if you're coming during the warmer months.** The market is placed in a sunny position, and it may become fairly hot.
- **Wear comfy shoes.** You'll be doing a lot of strolling around the market.

3. Markthalle Im Viadukt

Markthalle Im Viadukt is a covered market hall that is open every day. It is an excellent area to get fresh fruit, meats, cheeses, and other local items. You may also discover a choice of restaurants and cafés in the market hall.

Website: https://www.im-viadukt.ch/en/home/
GPS Coordinate: 47.3879° N, 8.5266° E
Location: Markthalle Im Viadukt is situated in the Viadukt, a former railway viaduct that has been turned into a marketplace. The precise location is Viaduktstrasse 31, 8001 Zürich, Switzerland.
Opening hours: The market is open Mondays through Saturdays from 9:00 a.m. to 8:00 p.m., and closed on Sundays.
What to expect: Markthalle Im Viadukt is a vast and bustling market hall with a broad range of vendors offering fresh fruit, meats, cheeses, fish, baked products, and prepared cuisine. You may also discover a range of restaurants and cafés, as well as a few pubs.

Here are some of the goods you may find at the market:
- Fresh produce: fruits, vegetables, herbs, and spices
- Meats: beef, hog, lamb, chicken, and fish
- Cheeses: Swiss cheeses, and others
- Seafood: fresh fish, shellfish, and caviar
- Baked goods: bread, pastries, and cakes
- Prepared foods: sandwiches, salads, and hot dishes
- Restaurants: a range of cuisines, including Swiss, foreign, and vegetarian
- Cafes: coffee, tea, and pastries
- Bars: beer, wine, and cocktails

How to get there:
- **By public transportation:** The nearest tram station is Hardbrücke, which is serviced by trams 4, 13, and 14.
- **By bus:** The nearest bus stop is Limmatquai, which is serviced by buses 31 and 62.
- **By foot:** Markthalle Im Viadukt is situated in the Old Town, thus it is a short walk from many of the significant sites, such as the Grossmünster and the Kunsthaus Zürich.

If you're traveling from outside of Zürich, you may take the train to Zürich Hauptbahnhof. From there, it's a short walk to the market.

Here are the directions from Zürich Hauptbahnhof:
- Exit the railway station and turn left onto Bahnhofstrasse.
- Walk for around 10 minutes till you reach Limmatquai.
- Cross the Limmat River and turn left into Hardbrücke.
- Markthalle Im Viadukt will be on your right.

Tips:
1. Be careful to negotiate with the merchants in the fresh vegetable kiosks. They're typically ready to offer you a decent bargain.
2. If you're seeking a certain meal, make sure to ask the sellers for suggestions. They're glad to assist you in locating the ideal stuff.
3. If you're hungry, make sure to sample some of the prepared cuisine at one of the restaurants or cafés. There are a range of selections to pick from, including classic Swiss cuisine and foreign cuisine.
4. Bring sunscreen and a hat if you're coming during the warmer months. The market is placed in a sunny position, and it may become fairly hot.

5. Wear comfy shoes. You'll be doing a lot of strolling around the market.

4. Teddy's Souvenir Shop AG
Teddy's Souvenir store is a souvenir store that offers a broad selection of Swiss souvenirs. You may get cuckoo clocks, Swiss army knives, chocolate, and other classic goods.
Phone: +41 44 261 22 89
Website: https://www.teddyssouvenirshop.ch/
GPS Coordinate: 47.3703° N, 8.5434° E
Location: Teddy's Souvenir Shop AG is situated at Limmatquai 34, 8001 Zürich, Switzerland. It is situated just below the Grossmünster church, in the Old Town.
Opening hours: The store is open every day from 10:00 a.m. to 08:00 p.m.
What to expect: Teddy's Souvenir store AG is a major souvenir store that offers a broad selection of Swiss souvenirs, including: Swiss chocolate: Switzerland is famed for its chocolate, so this is a must-buy keepsake. You may purchase chocolate in different forms and sizes, from plain bars to beautifully designed truffles.

- **Cuckoo clocks:** Another classic Swiss souvenir is the cuckoo clock. These clocks are recognized for their meticulous workmanship and their joyful cuckoo sound.
- **Swiss army knives:** The Swiss army knife is a multipurpose instrument that is excellent for daily usage. It is a favorite keepsake for both men and women.
- **Swiss watches:** Switzerland is home to some of the world's most renowned watchmakers. You may discover a large choice of Swiss watches to pick from, from budget to premium brands.
- **Heidi books:** Heidi is a classic Swiss children's novel about a little girl who lives in the Alps. You may purchase Heidi novels in many languages, and they make a terrific memento for kids.

- Other souvenirs: Teddy's Souvenir Shop AG also offers a range of other souvenirs, such as T-shirts, mugs, and magnets.

How to get there:
- The simplest method to get to Teddy's Souvenir Shop AG is by taking the tram to the Limmatquai station, which is serviced by trams 4, 11, and 15. From there, it is a short walk to the store.
- By foot: The business is situated in the Old Town, therefore it is readily accessible by foot from most sections of the city.

If you're traveling from outside of Zürich, you may take the train to Zürich Hauptbahnhof. From there, it is a short walk to the store.

Here are the routes from Zürich Hauptbahnhof (Main station):
- Exit the railway station and turn left onto Bahnhofstrasse.
- Walk for around 100 meters till you reach the Limmat River.
- Cross the river and turn right onto Limmatquai.
- The business will be on your left after a few meters.

5. Schweizer Heimatwerk
Phone: +41 44 222 19 55
Website: https://www.heimatwerk.ch/
GPS Coordinate: 47.5586° N, 7.5866° E
Location: Schweizer Heimatwerk has two branches in Zürich, one at Uraniastrasse 1 and the other at Bahnhofstrasse 2.
Opening hours: The Uraniastrasse branch is open from Monday to Saturday from 10:00 a.m. to 7:00 p.m., and the Bahnhofstrasse branch is open from Monday to Saturday from 10:00 a.m. to 8:00 p.m.

What to expect: Schweizer Heimatwerk is a non-profit organization that promotes Swiss craftsmanship. The shop carries a broad selection of Swiss-made items, including:
- **Wooden crafts:** From spoons and bowls to toys and furniture, Schweizer Heimatwerk provides a broad assortment of wooden crafts.
- **Textiles:** Schweizer Heimatwerk offers a range of textiles, including clothes, household textiles, and accessories.
- **Jewelry:** Schweizer Heimatwerk presents a collection of Swiss-made jewelry, including necklaces, earrings, and bracelets.
- **Ceramics:** Schweizer Heimatwerk offers a range of Swiss-made ceramics, including plates, bowls, and cups.
- **Glassware:** Schweizer Heimatwerk offers a range of Swiss-made glassware, including drinking glasses, vases, and bowls.
- **Other products:** Schweizer Heimatwerk also offers a range of other things, such as toys, kitchenware, and souvenirs.

How to get there:
- Uraniastrasse 1: This is the primary site and is situated in the Old Town. It is a short walk from the Grossmünster church and the Lindenhof hill.
- Bahnhofstrasse 62: This is a smaller site and is situated on Bahnhofstrasse, the major retail route in Zürich.

Here are the routes to go to each location:
Uraniastrasse 1:
- **By public transportation:** The nearest tram station is Urania, which is serviced by trams 4, 11, and 15.
- **By foot:** It is a short walk from the Grossmünster church and the Lindenhof hill.

Bahnhofstrasse 62:
- **By public transportation:** The nearest tram station is Bahnhofstrasse, which is serviced by trams 2, 4, 6, 7, 11, and 15.
- **By foot:** It is a short walk from the Paradeplatz, the major plaza in Zürich.

6. Confiserie Sprüngli

Confiserie Sprüngli was created in 1836 by David Sprüngli-Schwarzenbach. It is one of the oldest and most renowned chocolatiers in Switzerland

Phone: +41 44 224 46 46
Website: www.spruengli.ch
GPS Coordinate: 47°22'10.13" N 8°32'21.12" E
Location: Confiserie Sprüngli is situated in Bahnhofstrasse 21, 8001 Zürich, Switzerland. It is situated in the center of the city, only steps away from the Bahnhofstrasse, the major retail route.

What to expect: Confiserie Sprüngli is a high-end chocolatier that offers a broad selection of chocolates, pastries, and other sweets. They are recognized for their finely produced chocolates, which are prepared with the best ingredients.
Opening hours: The store is open Monday - Friday 8.00 to 12.00 / 13.00 to 17.00.

How to get there:
- **By public transportation:** The nearest tram station is Bahnhofstrasse, which is serviced by trams 2, 4, 6, 7, 11, and 15. From there, it's a short walk to the store.

If you're traveling from outside of Zürich, you may take the train to Zürich Hauptbahnhof. From there, it's a short walk to the store.

Here are the ways to travel to Confiserie Sprüngli from Zürich Hauptbahnhof:
- Exit the railway station from the main exit.
- Turn left and go along Bahnhofstrasse.
- Confiserie Sprüngli will be on your right, at number 21.

Tips:
1. Be sure to taste the Luxemburgerli, a typical Swiss pastry that is prepared with a delicate almond cream and topped with chocolate.
2. If you're searching for a particular present, make sure to check out the gorgeously packed chocolates.
3. If you're on a budget, make sure to visit the Confiserie Sprüngli outlet shop, which is situated in Sihlcity, Hardstrasse 201, 8005 Zürich.
4. If you're coming on the weekend, be prepared for huge queues. The store is quite popular, and it may become pretty packed.
5. If you're not sure what to order, ask the staff for ideas. They are highly informed about the items and can help you discover the ideal stuff.
6. If you intend on carrying a lot of chocolate with you, make sure to put it in a cold bag. The chocolate might melt if it gets too heated.
7. If you're searching for a unique keepsake, make sure to check out the Confiserie Sprüngli tea towels. They are fashioned of high-quality linen and are tastefully embroidered with the Confiserie Sprüngli trademark.

7. Ramseyer's Whisky Connection

Ramseyer's Whiskey Connection is one of the greatest whiskey stores in the city. Ramseyer's Whiskey Connection has been established for almost 40 years, and it's a favorite among whiskey aficionados from all over the globe. The store features a vast assortment of whiskies, from single malts to blends, from all around the globe.

Ramseyer's Whisky Connection was started in 1981 by Markus Ramseyer. It is one of the oldest and most recognized whiskey stores in Switzerland.

Phone: +41 44 557 95 66
Website: https://whiskyconnection.ch/
GPS Coordinate: 47.3635° N, 8.5338° E
Location: Ramseyer's Whisky Connection is situated at General-Wille-Strasse 8, 8002 Zürich, Switzerland. It is situated in the Old Town, only a short walk from the Grossmünster church.
Opening hours: The store is open from Monday to Saturday, from 10:00 a.m. to 6:00 p.m.

What to expect:
Ramseyer's Whisky Connection is a tiny, but well-curated boutique that offers a broad selection of whiskies, from single malts to blends, from all over the globe. They also sell a collection of whiskey accessories, like glasses, decanters, and books.

How to get there:
- **By public transportation:** The nearest tram station is Grossmünster, which is serviced by trams 4 and 15. From there, it's a short walk to the store.
- **By foot:** If you're coming from the Old Town, it's a short stroll to the store.

If you're traveling from outside of Zürich, you may take the train to Zürich Hauptbahnhof. From there, you may catch the tram to Grossmünster.

Here are the routes from Zürich Hauptbahnhof:
- Take the tram 4 or 15 to Grossmünster.
- Get off at the Grossmünster station.
- Walk for 2 minutes to Weinbergstrasse 15.

The employees at Ramseyer's Whiskey Connection are incredibly educated about whiskey, and they're delighted to assist you in locating the appropriate bottle for your taste. If you're not sure what you're searching for, they can offer you some suggestions. If you're a whiskey enthusiast, make sure to stop by Ramseyer's Whiskey Connection. It's a terrific location to locate a new favorite whiskey or to learn more about this delightful drink.

Tips:
1. The store is open from Monday to Saturday, from 10:00 a.m. to 6:00 p.m.
2. Be sure to test some of the whiskies before you purchase them. The team is pleased to provide you with samples.
3. If you're not sure what to order, ask the staff for ideas. They are highly educated about the whiskies and can help you pick the correct stuff.
4. If you're searching for a unique memento, make sure to check out the Ramseyer's Whisky Connection t-shirts and mugs.
5. The staff speaks English, so you don't have to worry about a language barrier.
6. The store is wheelchair accessible.
7. There is no parking accessible near the business, however, there is parking available in the neighboring neighborhood.

8. Weihnachtsdorf Christmas Market (Weihnachtsdorf beim Bellevue)
GPS Coordinate: 47.3658° N, 8.5461° E
Location: The Weihnachtsdorf is situated in Sechseläutenplatz, in front of the Zürich Opera House. (Sechseläutenplatz., 8001 Zürich, Switzerland)
Opening hours: The market is open from late November through December, from 11:00 a.m. to 9:00 p.m.

What to expect:
The Weihnachtsdorf is the biggest Christmas market in Zürich and features over 100 vendors offering Christmas decorations, presents, food, and beverages. There is also a Ferris wheel, a petting zoo, and a Christmas train.

Tips:
1. Try to come early, since the market may be congested.
2. If you're shopping for certain products, be careful to come early, since the best stuff tends to go fast.
3. If you're hungry, make sure to taste some of the cuisines at the market. Several vendors are serving traditional Swiss food, as well as other cuisine.
4. Bring sunblock and a hat if you're coming during the day.
5. Wear comfy shoes.
6. It is a famous tourist location, so it may become fairly busy, particularly on weekends.
7. The market is wheelchair accessible.
8. There is no parking accessible at the market, however, there is parking available in the neighboring neighborhood.

Here are various ways to go to the Weihnachtsdorf Christmas Market:
- **By public transportation:** The nearest tram station is Sechseläutenplatz, which is serviced by trams 4, 8, 11, and 15.
- **By water:** The market is also accessible by boat. The nearest boat port is Bürkliplatz, which is handled by the Zürichsee Schifffahrtsgesellschaft.
- **By car:** There is no parking accessible at the market, however, there is parking available in the neighboring neighborhood.

If you're traveling from outside of Zürich, you may take the train to Zürich Hauptbahnhof. From there, it's a short walk to the market.

9. Singing Christmas Tree Christmas Market
GPS Coordinate: 47.3751° N, 8.5399° E
Location: The Singing Christmas Tree is situated in Werdmühleplatz, in the Old Town (Werdmühle Pl., 8001 Zürich, Switzerland).
Phone: +41 44 422 00 06.
Opening hours: The market is open from late November through December, from 11:00 a.m. to 9:00 p.m.

What to expect:
The Singing Christmas Tree is a unique Christmas market that boasts a 15-meter (49 ft) tall Christmas tree that is decked with lights and speakers. The tree is used to transmit Christmas carols and other festive sounds. There are also around 30 vendors offering Christmas decorations, presents, food, and beverages.

Tips:
1. Be sure to come early, since the market may be congested.
2. If you're shopping for certain products, be careful to come early, since the best stuff tends to go fast.
3. Wear comfy shoes. You'll be doing a lot of strolling around the market.
4. It is a popular tourist site, however, it is not as busy as the Weihnachtsdorf Christmas Market.
5. The market is wheelchair accessible.
6. There is no parking accessible at the market, however, there is parking available in the neighboring neighborhood.

Here are various ways to get to the Singing Christmas Tree Christmas Market:
- **By public transportation:** The nearest tram station is Grossmünster, which is serviced by trams 4 and 15.
- **By water:** The market is also accessible by boat. The nearest boat port is Bürkliplatz, which is handled by the Zürichsee Schifffahrtsgesellschaft.

- **By car:** There is no parking accessible at the market, however, there is parking available in the neighboring neighborhood.

If you're traveling from outside of Zürich, you may take the train to Zürich Hauptbahnhof. From there, it's a short walk to the market.

10 Interesting Gifts You May Get In Zürich

1. Swiss chocolate: Switzerland is famed for its chocolate, therefore this is a must-buy keepsake. You may purchase chocolate in different forms and sizes, from plain bars to beautifully designed truffles. The best location to purchase Swiss chocolate is from a local chocolatier, such as Confiserie Sprüngli or Läderach. Prices vary from CHF 5 for a tiny bar to CHF 100 for a box of truffles.

2. Cuckoo clock: Another classic Swiss memento is the cuckoo clock. These clocks are recognized for their meticulous workmanship and their joyful cuckoo sound. The ideal location to purchase a cuckoo clock is at a classic Swiss souvenir store, such as Teddy's Souvenir Store AG or Schweizer Heimatwerk. Prices vary from CHF 100 to CHF 1000.

3. Swiss army knife: The Swiss army knife is a multipurpose instrument that is excellent for daily usage. It is a favourite keepsake for both men and women. The best location to get a Swiss army knife is in a department shop, such as Globus or Jelmoli. Prices vary from CHF 20 to CHF 200.

4. Swiss watches: Switzerland is home to some of the world's most recognized watchmakers. You may discover a large choice of Swiss watches to pick from, from budget to premium brands.

The ideal location to purchase a Swiss watch is from a watch merchant, such as Bucherer or Tissot. Prices vary from CHF 500 to CHF 50,000.

5. Heidi books: Heidi is a classic Swiss children's novel about a little girl who lives in the Alps. You may purchase Heidi books in various languages, and they make a terrific keepsake for children of all ages. The best location to purchase Heidi novels is in a bookshop, such as Teddy's Souvenir store AG. Prices vary from CHF 10 to CHF 30.

6. Swiss flag: The Swiss flag is a popular memento, and you can get it in several sizes and designs. The best location to purchase a Swiss flag is at a souvenir store, such as Teddy's Souvenir Store AG or Schweizer Heimatwerk. Prices vary from CHF 5 to CHF 20.

7. Swiss cowbells: Swiss cowbells are another favorite gift, and they come in a range of sizes and colors. The best location to purchase a Swiss cowbell is at a souvenir store, such as Teddy's Souvenir Store AG or Schweizer Heimatwerk. Prices vary from CHF 10 to CHF 50.

8. Swiss music boxes: Swiss music boxes are noted for their meticulous workmanship and their wonderful melodies. The ideal location to purchase a Swiss music box is in a classic Swiss souvenir store, such as Teddy's Souvenir Store AG or Schweizer Heimatwerk. Prices vary from CHF 50 to CHF 500.

9. Swiss crystal: Swiss crystal is noted for its purity and brightness. You may discover Swiss crystal in a range of goods, including figurines, jewelry, and decorations. The best location to acquire Swiss crystal is in a department shop, such as Globus or Jelmoli. Prices vary from CHF 50 to CHF 5000.

10. Swiss wine: Switzerland produces some fantastic wines, so this is a perfect keepsake for wine aficionados.

You may find Swiss wine in a wine store, such as Caves des Alpes or La Cave du Centre. Prices vary from CHF 20 to CHF 200 per bottle.

Tips for Getting the Best Deals

1. Shop during the off-season: The greatest time to shop in Zürich is during the off-season, which is normally from November to March. This is when you'll discover the finest prices on clothing, souvenirs, and other products.

2. Shop at local markets: There are several local markets in Zürich where you may get fresh fruit, meats, cheeses, and other locally-produced items. These marketplaces are a terrific location to discover unusual souvenirs and presents.

3. Look for deals and promotions: Many stores in Zürich offer sales and promotions throughout the year. Be sure to inquire about any discounts that may be available.

4. Bargain: It's fairly commonplace to bargain in Zürich, particularly in fairs and flea markets. Don't be scared to negotiate over the price of an item until you're delighted with it.

5. Use a shopping card: There are a few shopping cards available in Zürich that give savings at participating shops. The most popular shopping card is the SwissPass, which also gives savings on public transit.

6. Be mindful of the exchange rate: The Swiss franc is a strong currency, so be sure to factor in the exchange rate while you're shopping.

7. Visit the Christmas markets: The Christmas markets in Zürich are a must-visit for every shopper.

These markets are open from late November through December and provide a large range of Christmas decorations, gifts, and food.

8. Take advantage of student discounts: If you're a student, make sure to inquire about student discounts at participating shops. Many stores provide discounts to students with a verified student ID.

9. Shop in the early morning: Many establishments in Zürich give discounts to consumers who shop in the early morning.

10. Shop on weekdays: Shops in Zürich are often less busy and offer greater discounts on weekdays.

11. Don't be afraid to walk away: If you're not content with the price of an item, don't be scared to walk away. There are many more stores in Zürich where you may get the same item at a better price.

12. Buy in quantity: If you intend on purchasing a lot of products, try buying them in bulk. This may save you money in the long term.

13. Take advantage of free shipment: Many businesses in Zürich provide free shipping on purchases above a specific amount.

14. Follow your favorite stores on social media: Many businesses in Zürich provide discounts and promotions on their social media profiles.

15. Be patient: Shopping in Zürich might be a little daunting, particularly if you're not accustomed to the high costs. Be patient and take your time to uncover the greatest prices.

How to Avoid Tourist Traps

1. Avoid the most popular tourist destinations if you are on a budget: The most popular tourist spots are generally the most costly and congested. If you wish to avoid tourist traps, attempt to explore some of the lesser-known attractions in Zürich.

2. Be aware of costs: Tourist traps frequently demand more fees than other sites. Be careful to compare costs before you make a purchase.

3. Don't be scared to negotiate: In certain circumstances, it is permissible to bargain with merchants in Zürich. This is particularly true at marketplaces and flea markets.

4. Use public transportation: Public transit is an excellent method to navigate about Zürich and avoid tourist traps. It is also significantly cheaper than cabs and Uber.

Here are some particular instances of tourist traps to avoid in Zürich:

1. The Swiss National Museum: This museum is one of the most popular tourist attractions in Zürich, but it is also one of the most costly. Instead of the Swiss National Museum, visit the Kunsthaus Zürich. The Kunsthaus Zürich is a world-renowned art museum with a collection of approximately 40,000 pieces of art. It is far less costly than the Swiss National Museum and it is also situated in the Old Town.

2. The Lindt Home of Chocolate: This chocolate factory is a famous tourist site, but it is also highly pricey. If you want to experience Swiss chocolate, there are many alternative venues in Zürich where you may do so for a fraction of the price. Instead of the Lindt Home of Chocolate, visit Sprungli. Sprungli is a historic Swiss chocolatier that has been in business since 1836.

They provide a range of chocolates, pralines, and other delicacies.

3. The Grossmünster: This church is one of the most famous sights in Zürich, however, it may be rather crowded, particularly during high tourist season. If you wish to view the Grossmünster, try to arrive early in the morning or late in the afternoon. Instead of the Grossmünster, visit the Fraumünster. The Fraumünster is another renowned church in Zürich. It is less busy than Grossmünster and it also provides spectacular views of the city.

4. The Bahnhofstrasse: This is the major retail route in Zürich and it is full of pricey boutiques. If you're on a budget, try to avoid shopping on the Bahnhofstrasse. Instead of the Bahnhofstrasse, visit Niederdorf. The Niederdorf is a lovely old town quarter with small alleyways and a variety of shops and eateries. It is a nice spot to roam around and investigate.

I hope these ideas help you avoid tourist traps in Zürich and have a wonderful time visiting the city!

CHAPTER NINE

NIGHTLIFE IN ZÜRICH

Looking for an exciting night out in Zürich? You'll find everything here, from quaint pubs to hip clubs. So whether you're in the mood for dancing, drinking, or live music, you're guaranteed to have a wonderful time.

Lively Bars and Pubs

1. Widder Bar

There's a pub in Zürich that's so exclusive, it's only known by the locals and a select few visitors. It's called the Widder Bar, and it's one of the top bars in the world.

The Widder Bar is situated in the center of Zürich, in a lovely ancient building. The interior is sleek and sophisticated, with dark wood paneling and luxurious leather upholstery. The pub is recognized for its vast whiskey collection, having over 250 different varieties of whisky to pick from. They also offer an amazing assortment of drinks, wines, and beers.

The Widder Bar is the ideal spot to go for a special event or a night out with friends. The environment is cozy and the service is outstanding. And of course, the beverages are top-notch.

But be advised, the Widder Bar is not inexpensive. A drink will set you back at roughly CHF 20, and a glass of wine will cost around CHF 15. But if you're searching for a genuinely unique and unusual experience, the Widder Bar is worth it.

Here are some extra information regarding the Widder Bar:

Location: Widdergasse 6, 8001 Zürich, Switzerland
Phone: +41 44 224 25 26
GPS coordinate: 47.376807, 8.543322
Website: https://www.widderhotel.com/en/eat-drink/widder-bar
Menu: https://www.widderhotel.com/en/eat-drink/widder-bar/widder-bar-menue
Opening hours: 12:00 p.m. to 1:00 a.m. (Mondays - Thursdays). They shut around 2: 00 am on Saturdays, and 1: 00 am on Sundays
Reservations: Recommended, particularly on weekends
Entrance fee: None
What to expect: A stylish environment, superb service, and top-notch beverages
How to get there: The Widder Bar is situated in the center of Zürich, near the Bahnhofstrasse. It is readily accessible via public transportation.

- **By car:** From the A1 motorway, take the exit towards Zürich city center. Follow the signs for Bahnhofstrasse and then turn left onto Widdergasse. The Widder Bar will be on your right.
- **By public transportation:** Take the tram to the Bahnhofstrasse station. From there, travel south for approximately 50 meters and the Widder Bar will be on your right.

Estimated budget: CHF 100 per person for beverages and meal

Here are some helpful recommendations for visiting the Widder Bar:
- Dress smart casual.
- Be prepared to spend a little money.
- Make a reservation, particularly on weekends.
- Arrive early to avoid the throng.
- Enjoy the atmosphere and the beverages!

2. CP First Bar

Let's talk about CP First Bar, one of my favorite spots to go for a drink in Zürich. It's situated in the middle of the city, directly on the Limmat River. The pub features a mystical ambiance and a fantastic assortment of beverages, including beer, wine, cocktails, and spirits. They also offer a modest food selection, so you can get a bite to eat while you're there.

Here are some extra information regarding the CP First Bar:

Location: Schneggengasse 8, 8001 Zürich, Switzerland
Phone: +41 78 420 04 76
Website & Menu: https://www.cpfirstbar.ch/
Opening hours: The bar is open from 3 pm to 12 am, seven days a week. There's no cover fee, but it may become packed, so it's a good idea to make a reservation if you're coming on a weekend night.
Reservations: Recommended, particularly on weekends
Entrance fee: None
What to expect: When you enter CP First Bar, you'll be greeted by a friendly staff and a bustling ambiance. The pub is separated into two floors, with the main bar on the ground floor and a more private lounge space above. There's always something going on at CP First Bar, whether it's live music, DJs, or simply a nice talk with friends.
How to get there: CP First Bar is situated in Niederdorfstrasse 1, 8001 Zürich, Switzerland.
- From the Zürich Main Station, take the tram 4 or 11 to the stop "Niederdorf".
- Walk along Niederdorfstrasse for around 5 minutes till you reach the bar.
- The tavern is situated on the right-hand side, directly before the Grossmünster church.

Estimated budget: You may anticipate paying roughly CHF 20-30 per person for a drink and a little meal to eat.

Mode of payment: You may pay with cash or credit card at CP First Bar.

So there you have it, all you need to know about CP First Bar. I hope you enjoy your stay!

Dos and Don'ts:
- Do make a reservation if you're coming on a weekend night.
- Do order the trademark drink, the CP First.
- Do mix with the locals and make some new acquaintances.
- Do bring your ID if you're under 18.
- Keep your fur pets at home, please.

3. Rimini Bar

Rimini Bar is one of my favorite locations to go for a drink in Zürich. It's situated in the middle of the city, directly on the Schanzengraben. The pub provides a pleasant and relaxing ambiance with a wonderful assortment of beverages, including beer, wine, cocktails, and spirits. They also offer a modest food selection, so you can get a bite to eat while you're there.

Here are some extra information regarding the Rimini Bar
Location: Badweg 10, 8001 Zürich, Switzerland
Phone: +41 78 257 60 07
Website & Menu: https://www.rimini.ch/
Opening hours: The bar is open from 18:45 to 00:00, seven days a week. There's no cover fee, but it may become packed, so it's a good idea to make a reservation if you're coming on a weekend night.
Reservations: Recommended, particularly on weekends
Entrance fee: None
What to expect: When you enter into Rimini Bar, you'll be greeted by a friendly staff and a mellow ambiance. There's always something going on in Rimini Bar, whether it's live music, DJs, or simply a nice talk with friends.

How to get there: CP First Bar is situated in Niederdorfstrasse 1, 8001 Zürich, Switzerland.
- From the Zürich Main Station, take the tram 4 or 11 to the stop "Niederdorf".
- Walk along Niederdorfstrasse for around 5 minutes till you reach the bar.
- The tavern is situated on the right-hand side, directly before the Grossmünster church

Estimated budget: You may anticipate paying roughly CHF 20-30 per person for a drink and a little meal to eat.

Mode of payment: You may pay with cash or credit card at CP First Bar.

Dos and Don'ts:
- Do make a reservation if you're coming on a weekend night.
- Do order the trademark drink, the Rimini Spritz.
- Do mix with the locals and make some new acquaintances.
- Don't bring your kids or pets.

(PS. The legal drinking age in Switzerland is 18.)

4. Sablier, The Circle

Sablier is a rooftop restaurant and bar situated in The Circle, the new retail, office, and event area at Zürich Airport. It is the biggest rooftop restaurant in Switzerland and provides breathtaking views of the city and the Alps.

The restaurant features modern French cuisine, designed by chef Ronny Zipfel, who has been awarded 14 GaultMillau points. The menu contains meals such as roasted pigeon with foie gras and grilled scallops with cauliflower puree. There is also a big assortment of wines, including both French and Swiss wines.

The bar at Sablier provides a broad range of drinks, as well as a selection of spirits and wines. The bar crew is also glad to prepare special drinks to your satisfaction.

Sablier is a terrific venue to spend a nice dinner or to commemorate a particular event. It is also a popular venue for business meetings and gatherings. The restaurant is available for lunch and supper, and reservations are advised.

Here are some further details on Sablier:

Location: The Circle 23, Hangar D, 8058 Zürich Airport, Switzerland.
Phone: +41 (0)44 521 99 99.
Website: https://www.sablier.ch/.
Opening hours: Monday to Friday from 11:00 a.m. to 2:30 p.m., Saturday from 2 p.m. to midnight, and Sunday from 10 a.m. to 6 p.m.
Reservations: https://www.sablier.ch/en/reservation/

5. George Bar and Grill
George Bar & Grill is a rooftop restaurant and bar situated in the Haus Ober building in Zürich's Kreis 1 area. It provides amazing views of the city and the Alps.

The restaurant provides sophisticated European cuisine, with a concentration on grilled meats and seafood. The menu contains meals such as grilled octopus with chorizo and fennel salad and roasted duck breast with red cabbage and apple compote. There is also a big assortment of wines, including both Swiss and foreign wines.

The bar at George Bar & Grill provides a broad range of drinks, as well as a selection of spirits and beers. The bar crew is also glad to prepare special drinks to your satisfaction.

George Bar & Grill is a terrific venue to have a nice dinner or to commemorate a special event. It is also a popular venue for business meetings and gatherings. The restaurant is available for lunch and supper, and reservations are advised.

Here are some further details about George Bar & Grill:

Location: Sihlstrasse 50, 8001 Zürich, Switzerland.
Menu: george-grill.ch
Phone: +41 44 444 50 60
Website: https://www.george-grill.ch/
Opening hours:
Lunch: Tuesday to Friday from 11:30 am to 2:30 pm
Dinner: Tuesday to Friday from 5 pm to 12 am
Saturdays, 6 pm to 1 am
Bar: Tuesday to Saturday from 6 pm to midnight
They do not open on Sundays and Mondays.

6. Clouds
Clouds is a rooftop bar and restaurant situated on the 35th level of the Prime Tower in Zürich. It provides amazing 360-degree views of the city and the Alps.

The bar is recognized for its unique European-themed cocktails, which are crafted with fresh, seasonal ingredients. There is also a vast assortment of wines, beers, and spirits.

Cloud is a famous site for both residents and visitors. It is a terrific area to relax and enjoy the scenery, or to celebrate a particular event. The bar is open from Tuesdays to Saturdays, from 6 p.m. to midnight, and reservations are suggested.

Here are some further details on Clouds:

Location: It is situated in Prime Tower, Maagpl. 5, 8005 Zürich, Switzerland.
Phone: +41 44 404 30 00.

165 | Zürich Travel Guide

Website: https://clouds.ch/, You may make your bookings there.
If you are seeking a unique and unusual venue to have a drink in Zürich, Clouds is the right place for you.

Here are some recommendations for visiting Clouds:
- Make a reservation, particularly if you are traveling on a weekend.
- Dress smart casual.
- Be prepared to spend a premium on beverages and meals.

Trendy Nightclubs and Lounges

1. Hive Club

This is one of the most popular nightclubs in Zürich, and it is recognized for its electronic music and its dynamic atmosphere. The club includes three rooms, each with its own sound system and DJ booth. Hive Club organizes a range of events, including club nights, concerts, and parties.

Dress code: The dress code at Hive Club is casual chic. This implies that you should avoid wearing anything too revealing or too casual. Jeans and a good shirt are normally appropriate, but you may want to dress up a little more if you are going on a weekend night.

Age restrictions: The age limit for Hive Club is 18 years old.

Location: Hive Club is situated in Geroldstrasse 5, 8005 Zürich, Switzerland. It lies in the Zürich-West district, which is a popular location with a lot of pubs and clubs.

What they offer: Hive Club provides a range of electronic music, from house to techno. They also feature a huge dance floor, a VIP room, and a bar.

Opening hours: Hive Club is open from 11 p.m. to 9 a.m., exclusively from Thursdays to Sundays. Do not make the mistake of visiting there from Mondays to Wednesdays, please.

Price: The cover price for Hive Club is 30 CHF for men and 20 CHF for women. Drinks are also rather pricey, with beers beginning at 10 CHF and cocktails starting at 15 CHF.
Phone: The phone number for Hive Club is +41 44 271 12 10.
Website: https://www.hiveclub.ch/

Here are some more things to bear in mind before visiting Hive Club:
- It is a busy club, therefore it is important to come early, particularly on weekends.
- The queue might be lengthy, so be prepared to wait.
- There is a dress code, so be sure to dress correctly.
- The club may become fairly busy, so be prepared to dance close to other people.
- The beverages are costly, so be prepared to spend a little of money.

2. Icon Club
This club is situated in the center of Zürich, and it is recognized for its VIP tables and its trendy décor. Icon Club is a prominent nightclub situated in the center of Zürich. The club is open from 11 p.m. to 5 a.m., and it is a popular destination for both residents and visitors.

Dress code: The dress code for Icon Club is smart casual. Men are obliged to wear collared shirts and shoes, while women are expected to wear dresses or skirts that are at least knee-length.
Gate fees: There is a cover charge of 20 CHF for males and 15 CHF for women.
Age restrictions: The minimum age to join Icon Club is 18 years old.
Location: Icon Club is situated in Augustinerhof 1, 8001 Zürich, Switzerland.
What they offer: Icon Club serves a range of beverages, including cocktails, beers, and wines. They also offer a modest food selection.

Opening hours: Icon Club is open from 11 pm to 4 am, Friday and Saturday.
Price: Drinks at Icon Club are on the pricey side. A drink will normally cost approximately 20 CHF.
Phone: The phone number for Icon Club is +41 44 448 11 33.
Website: https://www.icon-Zürich.ch/

If you are searching for a fashionable nightclub with a stylish décor and a dynamic ambiance, Icon Club is an excellent alternative. However, it is vital to remember that the dress code is rigorous and the cover price is rather hefty.

Here are some suggestions for visiting Icon Club:
- Dress smart casual.
- Arrive early, since the club might get packed later in the night.
- Be prepared to spend a premium on beverages and meals.

3. Mascotte
GPS Coordinate: 47.3664° N, 8.5468° E
This club is a little more low-key than Hive or Icon, but it is still a popular location for locals and visitors alike. Mascotte is the oldest club in Zürich, and it has been functioning since 1916. It is situated in the Enge district, near to the lake. The club is recognized for its wide music schedule, which runs from hip-hop to funk, punk, rock, metal, and folk. It also includes live performances by well-known worldwide performers, as well as comedy and readings.

Dress code: The dress code for Mascotte Club is casual chic. Men are supposed to wear collared shirts and slacks, while ladies are expected to wear skirts or dresses that are not too short.

Gate fees: There is a cover price at Mascotte Club, which varies depending on the event. The cover price is normally approximately CHF 20-30 for adults.
Age restrictions: The age limit for Mascotte Club is 18 years old.
Location: Mascotte Club is situated in Theaterstrasse 10, 8001 Zürich, Switzerland.
What they offer: Mascotte Club provides a range of beverages, including beer, wine, cocktails, and spirits. They also offer a complete bar menu, which includes snacks, appetizers, and entrees.
Opening hours: Mascotte Club is open from 11 p.m. to 4 am, Thursday through Saturday.
Price: The prices at Mascotte Club are typical for Zürich. A beer will cost roughly CHF 8, a drink will cost around CHF 12, and a dinner will cost around CHF 20.
Phone: The phone number for Mascotte Club is +41 44 260 15 80.
Website: https://www.mascotte.ch/

4. Supermarket

Supermarket Club is a prominent nightclub in Zürich that is noted for its unique mix of music and its welcoming environment. It is situated in the Old Town, in a former industrial building that has been turned into a trendy club environment.

Dress code: The dress code for Supermarket Club is smart casual. Men are supposed to wear collared shirts and shoes, while ladies are expected to wear dresses or skirts.
Gate fees: The gate price at Supermarket Club varies depending on the event, however, it is normally approximately CHF 20. There is no age limit, however, you must be 18 or older to consume alcohol.
Location: Supermarket Club is situated in Geroldstrasse 17, 8005 Zürich, Switzerland. It is readily accessible via public transportation.

What they offer: Supermarket Club provides a range of beverages, including cocktails, beers, and wines. They also offer a modest food selection.
Opening hours: Supermarket Club is open from 7pm to 6am, Friday to Saturday.
Price: Drinks at Supermarket Club are normally approximately CHF 10-15.
Phone: The phone number for Supermarket Club is +41 44 440 20 05.
Website: https://www.supermarket.li/

Here are some more things to bear in mind before visiting Supermarket Club:
- The club may become pretty packed, so it is a good idea to arrive early.
- There is a stringent no-picture policy within the club.
- The club is cashless, therefore you will need to bring a credit or debit card.

5. Moods
This club is situated in the Seefeld neighborhood, and it is noted for its live music and its rooftop patio. Moods is a jazz club situated in the Schiffbau, a former industrial complex in Zürich's Seefeld area. It is noted for its live music, which comprises local and worldwide jazz performers.

The club has a capacity of 400 people and provides a range of seating choices, including tables, chairs, and a bar. There is also a tiny dancing floor.

The dress code at Moods is smart casual. Men are expected to wear collared shirts and closed-toe shoes. Women are obliged to wear dresses or skirts that are at least knee-length.

There is a cover fee for Moods, which varies depending on the event. The age limit is 18 years old.

Moods is open Monday to Saturday from 7:30 pm, and close by midnight on Mondays to Thursdays, while Fridays and Saturdays they shut by 4 am, then on Sundays, 6–11 pm.

The average price for a drink at Moods is 15 Swiss Francs.

Location: Schiffbauplatz, 8005 Zürich, Switzerland.
Phone: +41 44 276 80 00.
Website: https://www.moods.ch/en

Here are some more things to know about Moods:
- The club is situated in a popular location in Zürich, so it is simple to get there by public transit.
- There is a rooftop patio with great views of the city.
- The club provides a range of activities, including concerts, seminars, and DJ nights.
- It is a popular place for both residents and visitors.

If you are searching for a nice spot to enjoy live jazz music in Zürich, Moods is the ideal place for you.

Here are some recommendations for visiting Moods:
- Make a reservation, particularly if you are traveling on a weekend.
- Dress smart casual.
- Be prepared to pay a cover fee.
- Enjoy the song!

Music and Entertainment Venues

1. Volkshaus
GPS Coordinate: 47.3756° N, 8.5271° E
Volkshaus Zürich is a big performance hall and event facility situated in Zürich, Switzerland. It was erected in 1910 and has a capacity of 1,200 people. The hall is utilized for a variety of events, including concerts, plays, operas, and conferences.

Location: Volkshaus Zürich is situated in Stauffacherstrasse 60, 8004 Zürich, Switzerland. It is readily accessible via public transportation. The closest tram station is Stauffacher. Numerous tram lines stop at this station, including:
- **Line 3:** From Central Station, this route runs through the Old Town and up the hill to Stauffacher.
- **Line 4:** This line travels from Seefeld to Sihlcity, and it stops in Stauffacher on the route.
- **Line 11:** This line travels from Enge to Hardbrücke, and it stops in Stauffacher on the route.
- **Line 13:** This line travels from Wipkingen to Seebach, and it stops in Stauffacher on the route.

Once you are at the Stauffacher tram station, you will need to walk for around 5 minutes to reach Volkshaus Zürich.

Reservations: Reservations are not necessary for most events at Volkshaus Zürich. However, it is advised to reserve tickets in advance for popular events, since seats may sell out rapidly. Tickets may be bought online or at the box office.
Website: https://www.volkshaus.ch/
Phone: +41 44 242 11 55.
What sort of music or event is performed at the venue?
Volkshaus Zürich offers a range of events, including concerts, plays, operas, and conferences. The sorts of music performed at the venue vary depending on the occasion. However, the theater regularly accommodates performances of classical music, jazz, and rock music.

What is the size of the venue? Volkshaus Zürich has a capacity of 1,200 persons. This makes it a medium-sized arena. The size of the venue will affect the mood and the experience. If you are seeking a more intimate environment, you may want to consider a smaller location.

What is the capacity of the venue? This is vital to know if you are going to attend a popular event, since tickets may sell out rapidly.

What are the age restrictions? Some events at Volkshaus Zürich have age limits. It is necessary to verify the event listing for age limits before you attend.

What are the prices? The pricing of tickets for events at Volkshaus Zürich varies depending on the event. Tickets may be bought online or at the box office.

What is the dress code? There is no dress requirement for most events at Volkshaus Zürich. However, it is recommended to dress correctly for the occasion you are going to. For example, if you are attending a classical music event, you may wish to dress more professionally.

What are the transportation options? Volkshaus Zürich is readily accessible via public transit. The closest tram station is Stauffacher.

Opening hours: It change based on the event. However, the hall is normally open from 10 am until 2 am.

What are the additional facilities offered? Volkshaus Zürich features a bar and a restaurant. There is also a coat check accessible.

Extra tips:
- Arrive early to avoid large lineups at the ticket office.
- Dress properly for the occasion you are going to.
- Be considerate to other patrons and the venue.

Here are some of my own opinions regarding Volkshaus Zürich:

- I admire the diversity of events that are held in Volkshaus Zürich. There is something for everyone.
- I enjoy the size of the arena. It is big enough to host major gatherings, yet it is not so vast that it seems impersonal.
- The personnel at Volkshaus Zürich are nice and helpful.

2. Kaufleuten
GPS Coordinate: 47.3716° N, 8.5364° E
Kaufleuten is a historic landmark in Zürich, Switzerland. It was established in 1864 as a guildhall for the city's merchants and craftsmen. The structure was eventually turned into a performance theater and event facility. The music hall and the club are distinct venues inside the Kaufleuten complex. The performance venue is situated at Helvetiaplatz 1, 8001 Zürich, Switzerland, while the club is located at Pelikanpl. 18, 8001 Zürich, Switzerland.

The music hall is a bigger facility that can hold up to 1,200 people. It is utilized for a variety of events, including concerts, plays, and operas. The club is a tiny facility that may seat up to 300 people. It is utilized for concerts, DJ nights, and other events.

Location: Kaufleuten is situated in the center of Zürich, at Helvetiaplatz 1. It is readily accessible via public transportation. The closest tram station is Stauffacher.
Reservations: Reservations are not necessary for most events at Kaufleuten. However, it is important to secure a reservation for popular events, since tickets may sell out rapidly. Reservations may be made online or by phone.

Website: https://www.kaufleuten.ch/. The website includes information about future events, ticket pricing, and other vital topics.

Phone: +41 44 225 33 00

What sort of music or event is performed at the venue? Kaufleuten holds a range of events, including concerts, plays, operas, and conferences. The facility also contains a bar and restaurant, which are available to the public.

What is the size of the venue? Kaufleuten has a capacity of 1,200 persons. The facility contains a huge main hall, as well as a smaller side hall.

What are the age restrictions? There are no age limitations for most events in Kaufleuten. However, certain events may have age limitations.

What are the prices? The cost for events in Kaufleuten varies based on the event. Tickets may be bought online or at the box office.

What is the dress code? There is no dress requirement for most events in Kaufleuten. However, certain events may have a dress code.

Opening hours: Kaufleuten is open from 10am to 11pm, seven days a week.

Transit options: Kaufleuten is readily accessible by public transit. The closest tram station is Stauffacher.

Other amenities: Kaufleuten features a bar and restaurant, which are available to the public. The facility also offers a coat check and bathrooms.

Extra tips:
- Check the Kaufleuten website or social media accounts for the latest events and ticket information.
- Arrive early to avoid large lineups at the ticket office.
- Dress properly for the occasion you are going to.
- Be considerate to other patrons and the venue.

3. Rote Fabrik

GPS Coordinate: 47.3435° N, 8.5365° E

History: Rote Fabrik is a former factory in the Wollishofen suburb of Zürich, Switzerland. It was erected in 1892 and used to make silk. The factory was abandoned in 1940, and it was subsequently colonized by artists and activists. In 1972, the city of Zürich purchased the plant and transformed it into a cultural center.

Location: Rote Fabrik is situated in Seestrasse 395, 8038 Zürich, Switzerland. It is readily accessible via public transportation. The closest tram station is Hardbrücke.

Reservations: Reservations are not necessary for most events at Rote Fabrik. However, it is important to secure a reservation for popular events, since tickets may sell out rapidly. Reservations may be made online or by phone.

Website: https://www.rotefabrik.ch/. The website includes information about future events, ticket pricing, and other vital topics.

Phone: +41 44 485 58 58.

What sort of music or event is performed at the venue? Rote Fabrik provides a range of activities, including concerts, plays, art exhibits, and workshops. The theater is well-recognized for its alternative and experimental programming.

What is the size of the venue? Rote Fabrik has a capacity of 1,000 persons. The facility contains a huge main hall, as well as a smaller side hall.

What are the age restrictions? There are no age limitations for most events at Rote Fabrik. However, certain events may have age limitations.

What are the prices? The costs for events at Rote Fabrik vary based on the event. Tickets may be bought online or at the box office.

What is the dress code? There is no dress requirement for most events at Rote Fabrik. However, certain events may have a dress code.

Opening hours: Rote Fabrik is open from 11am to 1am, seven days a week.

Transit options: Rote Fabrik is readily accessible via public transit. The closest tram station is Hardbrücke.

Other amenities: Rote Fabrik features a bar and restaurant, which are available to the public. The facility also offers a coat check and bathrooms.

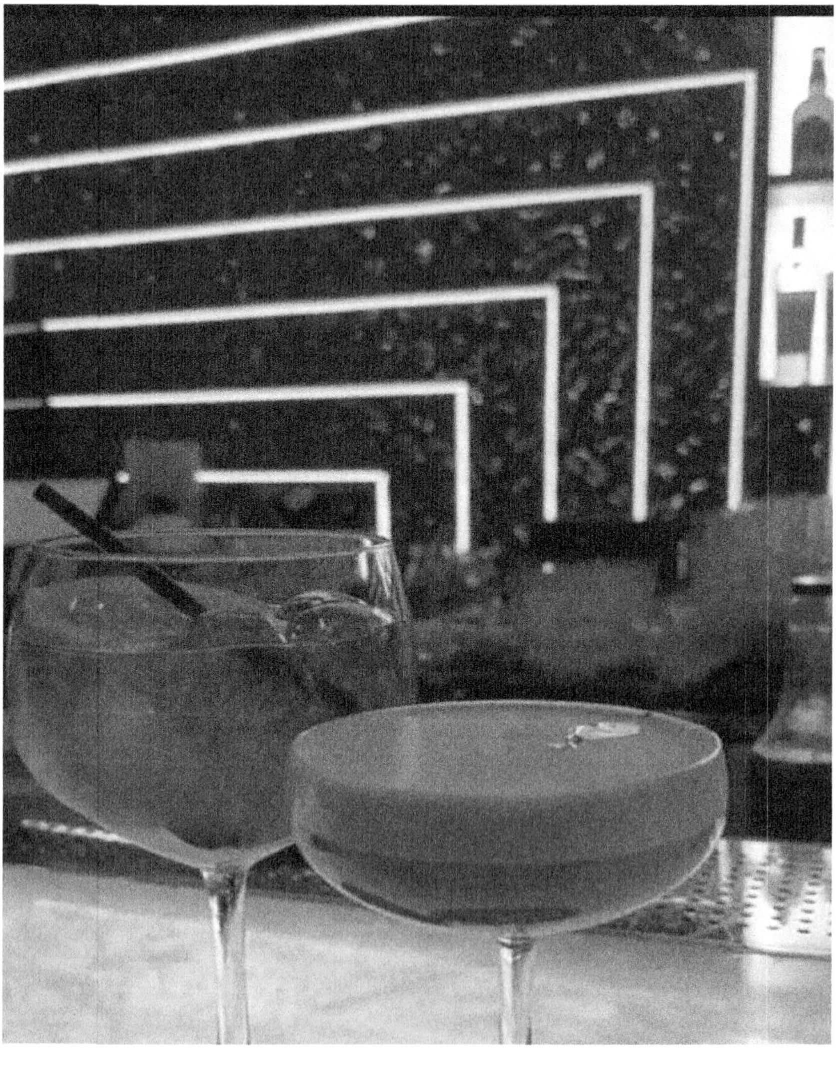

CHAPTER TEN

OUTDOOR ACTIVITIES AND NATURE

Parks and Gardens

1. Old Botanical Garden (Alter Botanischer Garten)
GPS Coordinate: 47.3712° N, 8.5338° E

The Old Botanical Garden is a 19th-century botanical garden situated in the city center of Zürich, Switzerland. It is home to a collection of approximately 8,000 plants from throughout the globe, including several rare and endangered species. The garden also features a variety of greenhouses, including a palm house and a fern house.

The park was created in 1837 by the University of Zürich. It was initially placed on the grounds of the university, but it was transferred to its present position in 1938. The garden is available to the public and is free to visit.

The Old Botanical Garden is a famous tourist site and is an excellent location to learn about plants and flowers. The garden is also a favorite area for rest and introspection.

Here are some extra information regarding the Old Botanical Garden:

Location: Pelikanstrasse 40 8001 Zürich, Switzerland
How to get there: The garden is situated in the city center, approximately a 10-minute walk from the major railway station.

You may also take the tram or bus to the ETH Hönggerberg station.
- By tram: Take tram number 2 or 9 to the ETH Hönggerberg station. From there, it is a short walk to the garden.
- By bus: Take bus number 31 or 81 to the ETH Hönggerberg stop. From there, it is a short walk to the garden.
- Walk out of the station and turn left onto Pelikanstrasse.
- The Old Botanical Garden will be on your right.

Contact: +41 44 634 84 61
Website: https://www.bg.uzh.ch/en.html
Opening hours: The garden is open from 7:00 a.m. to 7:00 p.m., from March to September. From October to February, it is open from 8:00 am to 6:00 pm. The tropical cottages are open every day from 9.30 a.m. to 4.45 p.m. The Cafeteria operates from Mondays through Fridays from 9 am-4 pm, while the library opens from 9 am-12.30 pm / 1.30-5 pm.
Admission fees: Free
Facilities: The garden features a variety of greenhouses, including a palm house and a fern house. There is also a playground, a picnic area, and a café.
Accessibility: The garden is wheelchair accessible.
Pets: Pets are not permitted in the garden because precious and rare plants grow everywhere.
Events: The garden organizes a variety of events throughout the year, such as concerts, festivals, and markets.

2. Chinagarten Zürich
GPS Coordinate: 47.3548° N, 8.5521° E
The Chinagarten Zürich was established in 1983 as a gift from the People's Republic of China to the city of Zürich. It is situated in the north of the city and is influenced by traditional Chinese gardens. The park has several pavilions, bridges, and ponds, as well as a diversity of plants and flowers.

Here are some extra information regarding the Chinagarten Zürich:
Location: Bellerivestrasse 138, 8008 Zürich, Switzerland

How to get there:
- **By public transportation:** The Chinagarten Zürich is situated near the Belleriveplatz tram station. You may take tram number 2, 4, or 7 to the Belleriveplatz station. From there, it is a short walk to the garden.
- **By car:** There is no separate parking lot for the Chinagarten Zürich. However, there is some street parking accessible in the vicinity.
- **By bike:** The Chinagarten Zürich is situated on the beaches of Lake Zürich. There is a bike route that follows along the lake, which is a wonderful way to get to the garden.

Here are the routes from the major railway station:
- Take the tram number 2 or 4 to the Belleriveplatz station.
- From the Belleriveplatz station, walk east along the lake for approximately 5 minutes.
- The Chinagarten Zürich will be on your left.

Contact: +41 44 380 31 51
Website: The Chinagarten Zürich does not have an official website. However, you may get more information on the garden here>>> https://www.stadt-zuerich.ch/ted/de/index/gsz/natur-erleben/park-und-gruenanlagen/parkanlagen-von-az/chinagarten.html

Opening hours: The Chinagarten Zürich is open from 11:00 am to 7:00 pm, from May to October. From November to April, it is open from 11:00 am to 5:00 pm.
Admission fees: Admission is free.

Amenities: The Chinagarten Zürich does not have any amenities, such as picnic spaces or BBQ grills. However, there is a tiny café situated near the entrance to the garden.
Accessibility: The Chinagarten Zürich is wheelchair accessible.
Pets: Pets are not permitted in the Chinagarten Zürich.
Events: The Chinagarten Zürich does not hold any events.

3. Pfingstweid Park
GPS Coordinate: 47.3879° N, 8.5128° E
The Pfingstweid Park was constructed in the 1990s as part of the reconstruction of the Zürich-West industrial region. The park is named after the Pfingstweid, a meadow that was utilized for grazing cattle during the Pentecost season.

Here are some extra information about the Pfingstweid Park:
Location: Pfingstweidstrasse 101, 8008 Zürich, Switzerland

How to get there:
- **By public transportation:** The park is situated near the Sihlcity shopping mall and can be accessed by tram or bus. The closest tram station is "Sihlcity", while the nearest bus stop is "Pfingstweidstrasse".
- **By automobile:** There is a car park available near the park, however, it might be congested during peak periods. The address of the car park is Pfingstweidstrasse 130, 8008 Zürich, Switzerland.
- **By bike:** The park is situated on the Zürichsee cycling route, which makes it a handy alternative for bikers.

Here are the routes from the major railway station:
- Take tram number 2 or 4 to the "Sihlcity" station.
- From the "Sihlcity" station, walk for approximately 5 minutes to the park.

Contact: +41 44 405 80 00

Website: The Pfingstweid Park does not have an official website. However, you may get more information on the park here>>> https://www.stadt-zuerich.ch/ted/de/index/gsz/natur-erleben/park-und-gruenanlagen/parkanlagen-von-az/pfingstweidpark.html

Opening hours: The Pfingstweid Park is open all day, every day.
Admission fees: Admission is free.
Facilities: The Pfingstweid district park features a spacious multi-purpose playground, a sunbathing spot, various seating options including benches and table/bench combinations, a playground equipped with a slide, swings, and a sandpit with a water pump, as well as amenities like table tennis tables, barbecue spots, a water basin, a drinking fountain, and accessible ZüriWC facilities.
Accessibility: The Pfingstweid Park is wheelchair accessible.
Pets: Pets are permitted in the Pfingstweid Park, however, they must be kept on a leash.
Events: The Pfingstweid Park organizes a variety of events throughout the year, such as concerts, festivals, and markets. It is a good idea to check the schedule of activities before going.

Here are some things to see and do in Pfingstweid Park:

The Japanese Garden: The Japanese Garden is a lovely and serene garden that is situated in the park. It is a popular site for weddings and other special occasions.
The Rose Garden: The Rose Garden is home to over 1,000 roses. It is a magnificent sight to view in the summer.
The Children's Playground: The Children's Playground is a nice location for youngsters to run about and play. It offers a variety of equipment, including slides, swings, and a climbing frame.
The Sports Field: The Sports Field is an excellent spot to play soccer, basketball, or volleyball. It is also a popular area for sunbathing.

The Dog Park: The Dog Park is a nice location for dogs to run about and play. It is fenced-in and contains a variety of obstacles for dogs to climb and jump on.

4. Quartierpark Schütze
GPS Coordinate: 47.3894° N, 8.5237° E
The Quartierpark Schütze Zürich was developed on the site of a former industrial school. The school, which was named the "Berufsschule Heinrichstrasse", was established in 1877 and dissolved in 1977. The structure was eventually utilized by the city of Zürich as a storage facility.

In 2004, the city of Zürich decided to rebuild the land of the old school into a park. The project was developed by the architectural company Jonas Wüest Architekten. Construction of the park started in 2017 and was finished in 2020.

The park is named for the Schütze family, who owned the property on which the school was erected. The Schütze family were initially farmers, but they eventually got interested in the textile business. The family's textile industry was situated on the site of the park until it closed in the early 20th century.

The park is also home to a lot of natural plants and trees, which give shade and beauty. The park is a popular site for people of all ages, and it is a terrific place to relax, play, and enjoy the outdoors.

Here are some extra information regarding the Quartierpark Schütze:
Location: Heinrichstrasse 240, 8005 Zürich, Switzerland
How to get there: The Quartierpark Schütze Zürich is situated at Escher-Wyss-Platz.
By public transportation:

- Tram: Take tram number 4 or 13 to the "Hardbrücke" station. From there, walk for roughly 5 minutes to Escher-Wyss-Platz.
- Bus: Take bus number 31 or 81 to the "Hardbrücke" stop. From there, walk for roughly 5 minutes to Escher-Wyss-Platz.
- Train: Take the S2 or S8 train to the "Hardbrücke" station. From there, walk for roughly 5 minutes to Escher-Wyss-Platz.
- By vehicle: There is a car park situated near Escher-Wyss-Platz, however, it might be congested during peak periods. The address of the vehicle park is Hardbrücke 4, 8005 Zürich, Switzerland.
- By bike: Escher-Wyss-Platz is situated on the Zürichsee cycling route, which makes it a handy alternative for bikers.

Contact: +41 44 412 52 14
Website: https://www.stadt-zuerich.ch/ted/de/index/gsz/naturerleben/park-und-gruenanlagen/parkanlagen-von-az/quartierpark-schuetze-areal.html
Opening hours: The Quartierpark Schütze Zürich is open all day, every day.
Admission fees: Admission is free.
Facilities: The Quartierpark Schütze Zürich is a contemporary park that is aimed to be a friendly and inclusive area for all people. The park features a range of amenities, including a playground, a sports field, a skate park, and a café. There is also a dog park situated on the perimeter of the park.
Accessibility: The Quartierpark Schütze Zürich is wheelchair accessible.
Pets: Dogs are permitted in the Quartierpark Schütze Zürich, however, they must be kept on a leash.

Events: The Quartierpark Schütze Zürich holds a variety of events throughout the year, such as concerts, festivals, and markets. It is a good idea to check the schedule of activities before visiting the park.

Some more advice for visitors and tourists visiting these parks and gardens:
- Be sure to wear comfortable shoes as you will be doing a lot of walking.
- Bring a water bottle since it might become hot in the summer.
- Take a map of the garden so you can easily find your way around.
- Be mindful of the environment and leave no evidence of your stay.

Lakeside Attractions

1. Zürichsee (Lake Zürich)
GPS Coordinate: 47.2225° N, 8.7527° E
Lake Zürich is the biggest lake in the canton of Zürich and the sixth-largest lake in Switzerland. It is situated in the north of Switzerland and is surrounded by mountains, notably the Uetliberg, which gives spectacular views over the lake and the city.

Zürichsee was created around 12,000 years ago when the glaciers that blanketed Switzerland receded. The lake has been utilized for transportation and pleasure for generations.

In the 19th century, Zürichsee became a famous resort for travelers. The first hotel on the lake was erected in 1837, and the first steamboat started running in 1855.

Today, Zürichsee is still a popular location for visitors and residents alike.

It is a gorgeous and attractive lake that provides a range of activities for people of all ages. Zürichsee is a popular area for swimming, boating, and sailing. There are also a lot of beaches and bathing spots surrounding the lake.

In addition to being a popular pleasure destination, Zürichsee is also an important transit hub. The lake is linked to the Rhine River by the Limmat River, and several ferries run on the lake.

Location and Transportation
Zürichsee is situated in the north of Switzerland. The closest large city is Zürich, which is situated on the eastern coast of the lake.

There are a variety of methods to travel to Zürichsee. You may take a train to Zürich and then walk or take a bus to the lake. You may also take a boat to the lake from Zürich or from other cities on the lake.
- **By boat:** Take a boat from the Zürich main station to one of the numerous docks on the lake
- **By tram:** Take tram number 11 or 13 to the "Bürkliplatz" station. The trip takes roughly 10 minutes.
- **By bus:** Take bus number 61 or 89 to the "Bürkliplatz" stop. The trip takes roughly 15 minutes.

Once you get to the "Bürkliplatz" station, walk for approximately 5 minutes to the lake. You will see the lake on your right-hand side.

The price for a single trip on the tram or bus is CHF 2.60. You may also purchase a day ticket for CHF 8.80, which is good for unlimited travel on any public transit in Zürich.

The lake is accessible all year round, but the ideal time to come is in the summer when the weather is pleasant and bright.

There are a variety of restaurants and businesses situated around the lake, so you can quickly find something to eat or drink.

Hours of Operation: The hours of operation for Zürichsee vary depending on the time of year. In the summer, the lake is open from dawn until sunset. In the winter, the lake is accessible from 10 a.m. until 6 p.m.

Facilities: There are a lot of amenities accessible at Zürichsee, including bathrooms, cafés, and stores. There are also a lot of beaches and bathing spots surrounding the lake.

Activities: There are several activities that you may enjoy in Zürichsee, including swimming, boating, sailing, fishing, and hiking. There are also a variety of festivals and events that are hosted on the lake throughout the year.

Tips
Here are some ideas for visiting Zürichsee:

1. The greatest season to visit Zürichsee is in the summer when the weather is pleasant and bright.
2. The fee for entrance to Zürichsee is free. However, there may be a fee for parking or activities, such as boating or sailing.
3. There are a variety of unique events and festivals that are hosted in Zürichsee throughout the year. Check the local calendar for further details.
4. There are several special events and festivals that are hosted on Zürichsee (Lake Zürich) throughout the year. Here are a few examples:

- **Zürich Pride celebration:** This celebration is held in June and honors the LGBTQ+ community. There are several activities, including a parade, a performance, and a party.

- **Street Parade:** This electronic music event is held in August and draws over 1 million people each year.
- This is a parade that takes place on the streets of Zürich, but it concludes at the lake, where there is a celebration and a fireworks show.
- **Zürich Film Festival:** This film festival is held in September and showcases a range of foreign films.
- **Caliente!:** This Latin American event is held in June and offers music, cuisine, and dancing. The Caliente! event takes place in the town of Wädenswil, which is situated on the beaches of Lake Zürich. The festival incorporates Latin American music, cuisine, and dance, and it frequently has activities that take place on the lake, such as boat parties or salsa dancing classes.
- **Züri Fäscht:** This event is held in July and highlights Swiss culture. This celebration involves a boat procession and a fireworks show on Lake Zürich.

The particular dates and timings of these events change from year to year, so it is important to consult the local calendar for further information.

Not all of these events happen on the lake itself. Some of them, such as the Zürich Pride Festival and the Zürich Film Festival, take place in the city of Zürich, but they frequently feature activities that take place on the lake, such as boat parties or concerts.

5. The difficulty level of the hiking routes surrounding Zürichsee varies. There are paths for all levels of expertise.
6. There are a lot of guided excursions offered for Zürichsee. This is an excellent method to learn more about the lake and its history. https://www.viator.com
https://www.getyourguide.com
https://www.zuerich.com/en/visit/nature/cruises-on-lake-Zürich

Safety Tips
Here are some safety measures that you should consider while visiting Zürichsee:
- Swim in approved places only.
- Be careful of the weather conditions and dress properly.
- Do not swim if the water is too chilly.
- Be wary of the currents and do not swim alone.
- Respect the local fauna.

i. The Zürichsee-Schifffahrtsgesellschaft (ZSG)
The Zürichsee-Schifffahrtsgesellschaft (ZSG) or Lake Zürich Navigation Corporation, established in 1837, is a public Swiss corporation operating passenger ships and boats on Lake Zürich and is the oldest shipping firm in Switzerland. It is a part of the Zürich Public Transport Network (ZVV) and carries about 1.5 million people every year. It runs a fleet of 17 vessels, including steamships, motorboats, and paddle steamers. The ZSG provides a range of services, including scheduled cruises, sightseeing trips, and private charters.

The ZSG plays a major part in the transportation system of Lake Zürich. It links lake-side settlements between Zürich and Rapperswil, as well as more tourism-focused excursions and boat services on the Limmat through the middle of the city of Zürich.

The ZSG is devoted to delivering a safe and enjoyable ride for its customers. The company's boats are outfitted with the newest safety measures, and the employees are educated to deliver exceptional customer service. If you are considering a vacation to Lake Zürich, I recommend you take a boat ride with the ZSG. It is a terrific way to explore the lake and the surrounding region and to enjoy the history and beauty of this lovely section of Switzerland.

ZSG Customer service: +41 44 487 13 33 & +41 44 487 13 13
ZSG Website: https://www.zsg.ch/en/timetable-prices
ZSG Address: Mythenquai 333, Postfach 8038 Zürich

Here are some of the services supplied by the ZSG:

Scheduled cruises: The ZSG conducts a variety of scheduled cruises on Lake Zürich, including sightseeing excursions, dinner cruises, and music cruises.

Sightseeing excursions: The ZSG provides a range of sightseeing trips on Lake Zürich, which enable you to experience the lake and the surrounding region from a fresh perspective.

Private charters: The ZSG also provides private charters for parties of up to 120 passengers. This is a terrific alternative for weddings, business celebrations, and other special occasions.

ii. Horgen–Meilen automobile ferry

The Zürichsee-Fähre Horgen–Meilen is a ferry service that runs between the cities of Horgen and Meilen on Lake Zürich. The boat is a popular method to move around the lake, and it also provides great views of the surrounding mountains and farmland.

The ferry service was originally started in 1932, and it has been in operation ever since. The present fleet consists of five ferries, all of which are powered by electricity. The boats are handicap accessible and include a lot of facilities, including bathrooms, restaurants, and stores.

The ferry service runs seven days a week, with a range of departure schedules. The travel between Horgen and Meilen takes roughly 10 minutes.

The Zürichsee-Fähre Horgen–Meilen is an excellent way to enjoy Lake Zürich. It is a pleasant and picturesque way to go about the lake, and it is also a terrific opportunity to visit some of the local sites.

Here are some particular details concerning how the boat service links to Lake Zürich:

1. The ferry service offers a handy means for passengers to go around the lake. It is a quicker and more picturesque choice than driving, and it is also a more inexpensive option than taking a cab or Uber.

2. The boat service provides spectacular views of the lake and the neighboring mountains. This is a terrific chance to observe the lake from a fresh perspective and to appreciate its beauty.

3. The ferry service is a famous tourist attraction. It is a terrific opportunity to explore the lake and learn more about the surrounding region.
Website: https://faehre.ch/

2. Mythenquai
GPS Coordinate: 47.3662° N, 8.5467° E
Mythenquai is a waterfront promenade situated in the Old Town of Zürich. It is a popular area for strolling, bicycling, and people-watching. The promenade provides spectacular views of the lake and the Grossmünster cathedral.

Mythenquai was constructed in the 19th century. It was originally named the "Quai zum Schiffslandeplatz", which means "quay to the landing stage". The name was changed to Mythenquai in the early 20th century. The name "Mythenquai" derives from the Mythen, a mountain range situated to the south of Zürich. The promenade is named after the Mythen because it affords views of the mountains.

Location and Transportation
Mythenquai is situated in the Old Town of Zürich. It is readily accessible via public transportation. The closest tram station is "Bürkliplatz". Here are the instructions on how to get to Mythenquai from the main railway station in Zürich:

1. Take the tram number 11 or 13 to the "Bürkliplatz" stop. The trip takes roughly 10 minutes.
2. From the "Bürkliplatz" station, walk for approximately 5 minutes to Mythenquai. You may also reach Mythenquai by taking bus number 61 or 89 to the "Bürkliplatz" stop. The trip takes roughly 15 minutes.
3. Once you get to the "Bürkliplatz" station, walk for around 5 minutes to Mythenquai. You will see the promenade on your right-hand side.

Hours of Operation: Mythenquai is open 24 hours a day, 7 days a week.

Facilities: Mythenquai offers a multitude of amenities, including bathrooms, restaurants, and stores. There are also a lot of seats where visitors can relax and enjoy the view.

Activities: There are a range of activities that visitors may enjoy in Mythenquai, such as walking, biking, people-watching, and taking photography. There are also a variety of restaurants and stores situated on the promenade.

Tips
Here are some recommendations for visiting Mythenquai:
1. The best time to visit Mythenquai is in the summer when the weather is pleasant and bright.
2. There is no entry cost to visit Mythenquai.
3. There are a variety of restaurants and businesses situated on the promenade, so you can quickly find something to eat or drink.
4. Be careful of the weather conditions and dress properly.

Safety Tips
Here are some safety measures that tourists should consider while visiting Mythenquai:

- Be alert of your surroundings and do not leave your valuables unattended.
- Be cautious while walking on the promenade, since it might be slippery when wet.
- Do not swim in the lake, since it is not safe.

Other Information
- The ideal time of year to visit Mythenquai is in the summer when the weather is bright and sunny.
- The cost of entrance to Mythenquai is free.
- There are a variety of unique events and festivals that are hosted on Mythenquai throughout the year.
- The difficulty level of any hiking routes in the region is easy.

There are a lot of guided excursions offered for Mythenquai.
- https://www.viator.com
- https://www.getyourguide.com
- https://www.zuerich.com/en/visit/nature/cruises-on-lake-Zürich

3. Quaibrücke
GPS Coordinate: 47.3668° N, 8.5431° E
Quaibrücke is a bridge that spans the Limmat River in the Old Town of Zürich, Switzerland. It is a famous site for shooting shots of the Grossmünster church and the river.

Quaibrücke was completed in 1886 and is one of the oldest bridges in Zürich. It was initially constructed as a railway bridge, but it is currently used by walkers and bicycles.

Location and Transportation
Quaibrücke is situated in the Old Town of Zürich, near the Grossmünster church. It is readily accessible via public transportation. The closest tram station is the "Bürkliplatz" stop.

Here are the stages in detail:
- Go to the main railway station in Zürich.
- Look for the tram station that reads "Bahnhofstrasse".
- Take tram number 11 or 13.
- Sit on the left-hand side of the tram so that you can view the lake.
- The tram will stop at the "Bürkliplatz" stop.
- Get off the tram and walk for around 5 minutes to Quaibrücke.
- You may also go to Quaibrücke by riding the bus. Bus number 61 or 89 stops at the "Bürkliplatz" stop. The trip takes roughly 15 minutes.

Hours of Operation: Quaibrücke is open 24 hours a day

Facilities: There are no amenities accessible at Quaibrücke.

Activities: The major pastime that visitors love visiting Quaibrücke is snapping photographs of the Grossmünster church and the river. You may also walk or bike over the bridge.

Tips
1. The ideal time to visit Quaibrücke is during the day when the light is wonderful for capturing photography.

Safety Tips
There are no unique safety problems at Quaibrücke. However, it is always a good idea to be alert to your surroundings and to take measures against pickpockets.

Special Events and Festivals: There are no unique events or festivals that are hosted exclusively at Quaibrücke. However, the bridge is a favorite site for spectators during the Street Parade, which is an electronic music event that is hosted in Zürich every August.

Cost of Admission: There is no payment to visit Quaibrücke.

Difficulty Level of Any Hiking Trails: There are no hiking paths near Quaibrücke.

Availability of Guided Tours: There are no guided trips that expressly visit Quaibrücke. However, there are a variety of guided excursions that give walking tours of the Old Town of Zürich, which includes Quaibrücke.

Hiking and Adventure Sports

1. Sihlwald
Telephone: +41 44 722 55 22
Sihlwald is a woodland situated in the north of Zürich, Switzerland. It is a popular place for hiking, biking, and camping. It provides a unique blend of woodland, wildness, and riverscape. The woodland is home to a variety of species, including deer, foxes, and owls. The park encompasses an area of 1,400 hectares and is home to a variety of species, including deer, foxes, and owls.

Sihlwald has been utilized for leisure for generations. In the 19th century, the woodland was popular with the city's affluent. Today, Sihlwald is accessible to everyone and is a popular attraction for residents and visitors alike.

Location and Transportation
Sihlwald is situated around 10 kilometers north of Zürich city center. It is readily accessible via public transportation. The closest railway station is Sihlwald station. From the railway station, it is a short walk to the forest entrance. **Alte Sihltalstrasse 38, 8135 Sihlwald.**

Hours of Operation: Sihlwald is open all year round. However, certain paths may be blocked throughout the winter months owing to snow. Mon – Sun: 9:00 a.m. – 12:00 p.m., 1:00 p.m. – 5:30 p.m

Facilities: Sihlwald includes a multitude of amenities for guests, including bathrooms, picnic spots, and a restaurant. There are also a lot of hiking routes and bicycle trails in the woodland.

Activities: The most popular activities in Sihlwald include hiking, biking, and camping. There are also a lot of other activities accessible, such as fishing, swimming, and horseback riding.

Tips
1. The greatest time to visit Sihlwald is during the spring or autumn when the weather is moderate. However, the forest is equally attractive in the winter, when the trees are blanketed with snow.

2. It is vital to be cautious of the weather conditions while hiking in Sihlwald. The forest may be hazardous in severe weather, therefore it is necessary to be prepared. It is also crucial to have suitable footwear and apparel while trekking in the forest.

Safety Tips
Here are some safety considerations to follow while hiking in Sihlwald:
1. Stay on approved paths.
2. Be mindful of your surroundings and look out for animals.
3. Bring lots of water and snacks.
4. Tell someone where you are going and when you intend to be back.
5. Be prepared for harsh weather.

Difficulty Level of Any Hiking Trails: There are several hiking paths in Sihlwald, with varied degrees of difficulty.

- The simplest hikes are suited for families with small children. The most demanding paths are appropriate for experienced hikers.

Some of the more popular hiking paths in Sihlwald include:
- The Sihlwald track: This is a 5-kilometer circular track that takes you into the heart of the forest.
- The Sihlsee route: This is a 4-kilometer route that follows the shoreline of Sihlsee Lake.
- The Uetliberg track: This is a 7-kilometer track that brings you to the summit of Uetliberg mountain, which gives beautiful views of Zürich.

Availability of Guided Tours: There are a lot of guided excursions offered in Sihlwald. These trips are a terrific opportunity to learn about the forest and its history. You may get more information about these trips and others on the website of the Wildnispark Sihlwald. The webpage of the Wildnispark Sihlwald is https://www.wildnispark.ch/en/

2. Pfannenstiel
GPS Coordinate: 47.2923° N, 8.6709° E

Pfannenstiel is a mountain situated in the north of Zürich. It is readily accessible via public transportation. The closest railway station is Uetliberg, which is a short walk from the peak of Pfannenstiel.

- **By rail:** Take the S10 or S24 train from Zürich Hauptbahnhof to Uetliberg station. From there, it is a short trek to the peak of Pfannenstiel.
- **By automobile:** There is a parking park at Uetliberg station. From there, it is a short trek to the peak of Pfannenstiel.

Hours of Operation: Pfannenstiel are open all year round. However, certain paths may be blocked throughout the winter months owing to snow.

Admission Fees and Where to Get Tickets: There is no entry cost to trek to Pfannenstiel. However, there is a parking charge at the Uetliberg railway station.

Facilities: There are a lot of amenities accessible at Pfannenstiel, including bathrooms, restaurants, and stores. There is also a mountain chalet at the peak, which sells food and refreshments.

Restrooms: There are bathrooms at the Uetliberg railway station and the peak of Pfannenstiel.

Eateries: There are various eateries near the Uetliberg railway station and at the peak of Pfannenstiel.

Stores: There are a few stores near the Uetliberg railway station offering gifts and hiking supplies.

Activities: The most popular activities in Pfannenstiel are hiking and mountain biking. There are a variety of paths of varied difficulty levels, ranging from simple to demanding. There is also a paragliding school in Pfannenstiel, which provides tandem flights for guests.

Hiking: There are about 100 kilometers of hiking routes in the Pfannenstiel region. The simplest hikes are suited for families with small children. The most demanding paths are appropriate for experienced hikers.
Mountain riding: There are about 50 kilometers of mountain bike routes in the Pfannenstiel region. The trails vary from simple to tough.
Paragliding: Paragliding is a popular pastime at Pfannenstiel. Several paragliding schools in the region provide tandem flights.

Tips
1. The ideal time to visit Pfannenstiel is during the spring or autumn when the weather is moderate.

However, the mountain is also magnificent in the winter, when the trees are covered with snow.

2. It is necessary to be careful of the weather conditions while hiking in Pfannenstiel. The mountain may be perilous in severe weather, therefore it is vital to be prepared. It is also crucial to have suitable footwear and apparel while trekking in the mountains.

- Weather: Check the weather forecast before you start trekking.
- Footwear: Wear sturdy hiking boots or shoes.
- Clothes: Wear layers of clothes so that you can adapt to the weather.
- Food and water: Bring lots of food and water.
- Sunscreen: Wear sunscreen, especially on overcast days.
- Insect spray: Bring insect spray, particularly if you are trekking in the summer.

Safety Tips
Here are some safety considerations to follow while hiking in Pfannenstiel:
- Stay on approved paths.
- Be mindful of your surroundings and look out for animals.
- Bring lots of water and snacks.
- Tell someone where you are going and when you intend to be back.
- Be prepared for harsh weather.

Special Events and Festivals
There are a variety of unique events and festivals hosted at Pfannenstiel throughout the year. The most popular event is the Pfannenstiel Mountain Festival, which is held in July. The event contains a range of activities, such as music, and cuisine.

3. Uetliberg
GPS Coordinate: 47.3495° N, 8.4920° E

Among the interesting hiking and adventure sports areas, Uetliberg stands out as a favorite among tourists and first-timers seeking a nature-filled vacation. Situated within a short distance from the city center, Uetliberg provides a fantastic blend of magnificent surroundings and adrenaline activities. Uetliberg is a mountain overlooking Zürich. It is a popular area for hiking, bicycling, and picnics. There is also a café and an observation deck at the summit of the mountain.

The history of Uetliberg is connected with Zürich's passion for nature. Once a peaceful woodland location, Uetliberg became a favorite destination in the 19th century as hiking acquired popularity as a leisure activity. Today, its value as a natural sanctuary adjacent to the urban core remains strong.

Location and Transportation
Accessing Uetliberg is convenient. Travelers may select public transportation, including trains or buses, to reach the Uetliberg mountain region. Alternatively, people with their automobiles may park at authorized parking areas nearby.

Hours of Operation: Uetliberg's trails and adventure places are normally available year-round, allowing for exploration throughout various seasons. It's important to check for particular trail closures and time restrictions on the official website.

Admission Fees & Where to Get Tickets: Uetliberg's natural splendor and trails are accessible free of charge, making it an inexpensive destination for outdoor lovers. No entrance tickets are needed.

Amenities: Visitors to Uetliberg may enjoy well-maintained amenities, including clean bathrooms, shops serving food and drinks, and picnic sites. These facilities create a pleasant experience for adults and families alike.

Activities: Uetliberg offers a varied spectrum of adventure enthusiasts. Hiking is the highlight, with several paths catering to different ability levels. Mountain biking, trail running, and even paragliding are popular sports that add to the thrill.

Tips
1. Wear good hiking shoes and weather-appropriate attire.
2. Bring along sunscreen, a drink, and a map of the trails.
3. Expect changeable weather conditions, so be prepared for rain or rapid temperature fluctuations.

Safety Tips
- Safety is vital when enjoying Uetliberg's paths. Stay updated on weather forecasts and trail conditions.
- Adequate footwear is vital for stability during treks, and observing trail regulations helps avoid accidents.
- Uetliberg's paths may become treacherous during wet or snowy circumstances. Stay vigilant and alter your plans appropriately.

Special Activities and Festivals: Uetliberg periodically holds activities such as guided nature walks, astronomy evenings, and local festivals enjoying the outdoors. Check the official website for event scheduling.

Cost of entrance: Free entrance for all guests.

Difficulty Level of Hiking Paths: Uetliberg provides an assortment of paths, ranging from simple to moderate and somewhat tough. Some noteworthy trails include:
- **Uetliberg Panorama Trail:** Easy, good for families with children.
- **Felsenegg Trail:** Moderate, with excellent perspectives.
- **Uetliberg Loop Trail:** Moderate to challenging, suggested for experienced hikers.

Availability of Guided Tours: Guided tours are provided for individuals interested in a better knowledge of Uetliberg's environment, history, and geology. Check the official website for tour choices.

Best Way to Get There: Take a short train or bus trip from Zürich's main station to Uetliberg station, and from there, it's a lovely stroll to the mountain's paths.

Website: For additional information, trail maps, and updates, see the official Uetliberg website: www.uctliberg.ch

4. Männlichen
GPS Coordinate: 46° 36' 57.42" N and 7° 54' 54.792" E
Männlichen is a mountain situated in the Bernese Oberland, approximately 10 kilometers from Interlaken. It is a popular area for hiking, skiing, and snowboarding. The trek to Männlichen is tough and takes roughly 4 to 5 hours. The path is not as well-maintained as the trails to Uetliberg and Felsegg, but it is still achievable with adequate clothing and planning.

Location and Transportation
It is readily accessible via public transportation. The closest railway station is Grindelwald, from whence there is a cable car to Männlichen.

- By rail: Take the Interlaken Ost to Grindelwald Grund train. From there, take the Männlichenbahn cable car to Männlichen.

Hours of Operation: Männlichen are open all year round. However, certain paths may be blocked throughout the winter months owing to snow.

Admission Fees and Where to Get Tickets: There is no entry cost to trek to Männlichen.

However, there is a cost for the cable car journey. Tickets may be bought online or at the ticket office in Grindelwald.

Facilities: There are a lot of amenities accessible at Männlichen, including bathrooms, restaurants, and stores. There is also a mountain chalet at the peak, which sells food and refreshments.

Bathrooms: There are bathrooms at the cable car station and the peak of Männlichen.
Restaurants: There are various restaurants at the top of Männlichen, serving a range of cuisine and beverages.
Stores: There are a few stores at the peak of Männlichen offering gifts and hiking supplies.

Activities: The most popular activities in Männlichen are hiking and mountain biking. There are a variety of paths of varied difficulty levels, ranging from simple to demanding. There is also a paragliding school in Männlichen, which provides tandem flights.

Hiking: There are about 100 kilometers of hiking paths in the Männlichen region. The simplest hikes are suited for families with small children. The most demanding paths are appropriate for experienced hikers.

Mountain riding: There are about 50 kilometers of mountain bike routes in the Männlichen region. The trails vary from simple to tough.

Paragliding: Paragliding is a popular pastime in Männlichen. Several paragliding schools in the region provide tandem flights.

Tips
1. The ideal time to visit Männlichen is during the spring or autumn when the temperature is moderate. However, the mountain is also magnificent in the winter, when the trees are covered with snow.

2. It is necessary to be careful of the weather conditions while hiking in Männlichen. The mountain may be perilous in severe weather, therefore it is vital to be prepared. It is also crucial to have suitable footwear and apparel while trekking in the mountains.

- **Weather:** Check the weather forecast before you start trekking.
- **Footwear:** Wear sturdy hiking boots or shoes.
- **Clothes:** Wear layers of clothes so that you can adapt to the weather.
- **Food and water:** Bring lots of food and water.
- **Sunscreen:** Wear sunscreen, especially on overcast days.
- **Insect spray:** Bring insect spray, particularly if you are trekking in the summer.

Safety Tips
Here are some safety considerations to follow while hiking in Männlichen:
- Stay on approved paths.
- Be mindful of your surroundings and look out for animals.
- Bring lots of food and drink.
- Tell someone where you are going and when you intend to be back.
- Be prepared for harsh weather.

Special Events and Festivals: There are a variety of unique events and festivals hosted at Männlichen throughout the year. The most popular event is the Männlichen Mountain Festival, which is held annually in July. The event contains a range of activities, such as music, cuisine, and games.
Website: Männlichen: https://www.maennlichen.ch/en/

Difficulty Level of Any Hiking Trails: The difficulty level of the paths in the Männlichen region varies. Some of the simplest trails include the Faulhorn.

The Environmental Effect of Hiking and Adventure Sports

Hiking and adventure sports may have a beneficial influence on the environment by increasing physical activity and decreasing pollution. However, they may also have a detrimental influence by disturbing animals, littering, and harming plants. It is crucial to be aware of the environmental effects of these actions and take measures to mitigate them.

Some techniques to lessen the environmental effect of hiking and adventure sports include:
- Choosing pathways that are less popular to prevent upsetting animals.
- Littering correctly and packing up all garbage.
- Avoiding activities that harm plants, such as off-trail hiking.
- Educating people on the necessity of respecting the environment.

The Necessity of Respecting Local Culture & Traditions

When hiking and adventure sports in a new location, it is necessary to respect the local culture and traditions. This involves being informed of the local rules and regulations, respecting private property, and wearing accordingly. It is also crucial to be cognizant of the influence of your actions on the local community.

Some approaches to respect the local culture and traditions include:

- Learning about the local culture before you travel.
- Asking permission before visiting private property.
- Dressing correctly for the local climate and culture.
- Spending money locally to assist the community.
- Being attentive to the influence of your actions on the surrounding environment.

Adventure Sports for Tourist In Zürich

1. Hiking: There are several hiking paths in and around Zürich, ranging from simple to hard. Some popular hiking sites include Uetliberg, Rigi, and Titlis.

2. Mountain biking: There are also several mountain riding paths in the vicinity, appropriate for all levels of expertise. Some prominent mountain riding sites include Uetliberg.

3. Paragliding: Paragliding is a popular pastime in the Swiss Alps, and numerous businesses provide tandem flights. Some popular paragliding destinations are Uetliberg, Rigi, and Titlis.

4. Rock climbing: There are several rock climbing sites in the Swiss Alps, ranging from basic to hard. Some popular rock climbing destinations are **the Eiger**, the Matterhorn, and the Jungfrau.

The Eiger is a peak situated in the Bernese Alps, roughly 2 hours from Zürich. It is one of the most renowned mountains in the world and is recognized for its demanding rock-climbing routes.

The Eiger features three major faces: the North Face, the East Face, and the West Face. The North Face is the most renowned and is regarded to be one of the most challenging rock climbs in the world. It has been climbed by just a few hundred individuals. The East Face is less difficult than the North Face but is still a tough climb. The West Face is the simplest of the three faces but is still a hard ascent for experienced climbers.

There are numerous different rock climbing routes on the Eiger, ranging from basic to tough. Some of the most popular routes are the North Face Direct, the Heckmair Route, and the Rotpunkt Route. If you are interested in rock climbing on the Eiger, it is vital to be experienced and in excellent physical shape. You should also hire a guide since the climbs are exceedingly risky.

Here are the methods to go to the Eiger:
- **By car:** From Zürich, take the A8 road to the Grindelwald exit. Follow the signs to Grindelwald and then to the Eigernordwand. There is a car park at the Eigernordwand.
- **By rail:** Take the Interlaken Ost to Grindelwald Grund train. From Grindelwald Grund, take the Grindelwald–Männlichen cable car to Männlichen. From Männlichen, it is a 20-minute walk to the Eigernordwand.
- **By bus:** Take bus number 1 from Grindelwald station to Alpiglen. From Alpiglen, it is a 15-minute walk to the Eigernordwand.

Once you get to the Eigernordwand, there is a reception center where you may acquire information about the climbs and hire a guide.

Here are some further details on the Eiger:
- The Eiger is 3,970 meters (12,966 ft) tall.
- The first person to climb the North Face of the Eiger was Heinrich Harrer in 1938.
- The Eiger has been the site of countless mishaps, including several fatalities.
- If you are seeking a tough and rewarding rock climbing adventure, the Eiger is a terrific alternative. However, it is crucial to be aware of the hazards associated and to take all required measures.

5. White-water rafting: White-water rafting is an exciting sport that may be experienced on the various rivers in the Swiss Alps. Some popular white-water rafting destinations are the Aare River, the Reuss River, and **the Rhine River.**

The Rhine River is a famous place for white water rafting in Zürich. It is a tough river with a variety of rapids, ranging from class II to class IV. The greatest season to go white water rafting on the Rhine River is during the spring and autumn, when the water levels are high. The river is also available for rafting in the summer, although the water levels are lower and the rapids are not as severe.

Here are the methods to get to the Rhine River for white water rafting in Zürich:
- **By car:** From Zürich, follow the A1 highway to the Rüti exit. Follow the signs to Altikon and then to the Rhine River. There is a parking park at the rafting company.
- **By rail:** Take the S24 train from Zürich Hauptbahnhof to Rüti station. From Rüti station, it is a 10-minute walk to the Rhine River.
- **By bus:** Take the bus number 647 from Zürich Hauptbahnhof to Altikon station. From Altikon station, it is a 5-minute walk to the Rhine River.

Once you get to the Rhine River, there will be signs pointing you to the rafting businesses.

There are a lot of different rafting businesses that operate on the Rhine River. Some of the most popular businesses include:
- SwissRaft
- Outdoor Interlaken
- Rafting Center Walensee

When picking a rafting business, it is crucial to examine the expertise level of the participants and the sort of rafting experience that they are seeking.

The cost of white water rafting on the Rhine River varies based on the operator and the duration of the trip. Prices normally start at CHF 100 per person for a half-day tour.

Here are some safety guidelines for white water rafting:
- Always wear a life jacket.
- Listen to the directions of the guide.
- Do not swim in the river unless told to do so by the guide.
- Be mindful of your surroundings and look out for pebbles and other dangers.

If you are searching for an exciting and demanding white water rafting trip, the Rhine River is a terrific alternative. However, it is crucial to be aware of the hazards associated and to take all required measures.

6. Caving: There are several caverns in the Swiss Alps, some of which are available to the public for exploration. Some popular caving places are the **Hölloch Caves**, the Blausee Caves, and the St. Beatus Caves.

The Hölloch Caves are the biggest cave system in Switzerland, with approximately 200 kilometers of excavated channels. They are situated in the municipality of Muotathal, around an hour's drive from Zürich. The caverns are a famous location for cavers and adventure lovers. There are several tours offered, ranging from simple to hard. The simplest trips are suited for families with small children. They lead guests through some of the most accessible portions of the cave system.

The most strenuous trips take guests further into the cave system. These excursions need participants to be in decent physical condition and to have some expertise with caving. All tours of the Hölloch Caves are guided by expert guides.

The guides offer safety equipment and education, and they guarantee that all participants have a safe and pleasurable experience. The Hölloch Caves are an interesting and attractive site to explore. They give a unique chance to discover the subterranean world of Switzerland.

There are various methods to go to the Hölloch Caves.
- **By car:** From Zürich, follow the A3 highway to the Muotathal exit. Follow the signs to Muotathal and then to the Hölloch Caves. There is a parking park near the cave entrance.
- **By rail:** Take the S24 train from Zürich Hauptbahnhof to Muotathal station. From Muotathal station, it is a 10-minute walk to the Hölloch Caves.
- **By bus:** Take bus number 84 from Schwyz station to Muotathal. From Muotathal bus station, it is a 10-minute walk to the Hölloch Caves.

Once you get to the Hölloch Caves, there is a reception area where you can buy tickets and obtain information about the excursions.

The webpage of the Hölloch Caves is: https://www.trekking.ch/hoelloch

Here are some further details you may discover on their website:
Opening hours: The caverns are accessible all year round, however, certain trips are only offered at particular seasons of the year.
Tickets: Tickets may be bought online or at the cave entrance.
Dress code: Participants are asked to wear comfortable clothes and shoes that they do not mind getting soiled.
Age limitations: There are no age restrictions for the simpler trips, however, the more strenuous tours need participants to be at least 12 years old.

Physical requirements: The simplest trips are suited for persons of all fitness levels, while the more strenuous tours need participants to be in excellent physical shape.

Here are some further details on the Hölloch Caves:
- The caverns were found in 1875 by a group of local farmers.
- The word Hölloch means "hell hole" in German.
- The caverns are made mainly of limestone and dolomite.
- The temperature in the caverns remains constant at 8 degrees Celsius (46 degrees Fahrenheit).
- The caverns are home to a variety of fauna, including bats, spiders, and cave salamanders.

7. Winter sports: In the winter, there are numerous options for skiing, snowboarding, and other winter sports in the Swiss Alps. Some popular ski destinations are Zermatt, St. Moritz, and Davos.

Rules & Restrictions for Fishing and Swimming In Zürich

Fishing
1. Fishing is legal in all public waterways in Zürich, save for the Limmat River in the city center.
2. A fishing license is necessary for all anglers above the age of 16. Permits may be obtained online or at any fishing equipment store. https://epeche.apps.vs.ch/shop
3. The daily catch limit is 3 fish per person.
4. There are several restricted places where fishing is forbidden, such as spawning grounds and near dams.
5. It is crucial to be informed of the local legislation and to preserve the environment.

Swimming
1. Swimming is legal in most lakes and rivers in Zürich.
2. Swimming is forbidden in the Limmat River in the city center.

3. Swimming is also restricted in several lakes and rivers that are utilized for drinking water.
4. It is crucial to be informed of the local legislation and to swim in safe locations.

Here are some extra permits and requirements to bear in mind:
1. If you are fishing in a private lake or river, you will need to seek permission from the proprietor.
2. If you are swimming in a lake or river that is utilized for drinking water, you should avoid swimming near the intake pipes.
3. It is forbidden to fish or swim in locations that are labeled as off-limits.
4. It is crucial to be aware of the hazards of swimming in cold water, such as hypothermia.

Day Trips and Excursions

If you're searching for a day excursion out of the city, you've come to the correct spot. There is something for everyone, from the high peaks of the Alps to the beautiful towns of Appenzell. So whether you're a thrill-seeker or a history buff, I've got you covered. And don't worry, we'll keep things light and enjoyable along the way. Here are some particular day tours and activities that I would suggest for first-timers in Zürich:

Scenic Swiss Villages

1. Appenzell: Appenzell is a picturesque area in northeastern Switzerland, noted for its quaint towns, rolling hills, and spectacular alpine views. The two half-cantons of Appenzell Innerrhoden and Appenzell Ausserrhoden are home to a rich cultural legacy, including traditional Swiss music, dance, and crafts.

Here are some of the activities you can do in Appenzell:

1. Visit the capitol, Appenzell, and discover the Old Town, with its colorful homes and tiny lanes.
2. Take a stroll or trek in the neighboring area and enjoy the breathtaking views of the Alps.
3. Visit a cheese factory and learn about how Appenzeller cheese is manufactured. Sample some of the local delicacies, such as Appenzeller sausage and Appenzeller cheese. https://appenzellerland.ch/en/
4. Go skiing or snowboarding in the winter.

To travel to Appenzell from Zürich, you may use the train. The trip takes roughly 2 hours. The train leaves from Zürich HB (major railway station) and arrives at Appenzell station.
The precise instructions are as follows:
- From Zürich HB, take the train to Gossau.
- Change trains at Gossau and take the train to Appenzell.
- The train timetable may be obtained on the Swiss Federal Railways website. https://www.sbb.ch/en

You may acquire your ticket and card here: https://www.sbb.ch/en/travelcards-and-tickets/tickets-for-switzerland/individual-tickets.html

The cost of the railway ticket is roughly 30 Swiss francs (around USD 30).

Here are some helpful recommendations for arranging your day trip to Appenzell:
1. The greatest time to visit Appenzell is during the spring or autumn when the weather is moderate.
2. If you are intending on hiking, make sure to wear comfortable shoes and carry lots of water.
3. There are several restaurants in Appenzell providing typical Swiss fare. Be sure to taste some of the local specialties!

4. If you are traveling with children, make sure to visit the Appenzell Children's Museum.

2. **Lauterbrunnen:** Tucked away in a deep valley, Lauterbrunnen is a picturesque hamlet in the Swiss Alps, noted for its stunning waterfalls and towering peaks, it's an outdoor enthusiast's ideal. The town is situated in the Bernese Oberland area of Switzerland, approximately a 2-hour train trip from Zürich.

Here are some of the activities you can do in Lauterbrunnen:

1. Hike to the Trummelbach Falls, a set of 16 waterfalls that flow into a cave system.
2. Visit the Staubbach Falls, the highest waterfall in the area, which plunges 300 meters (984 ft) over a rock face.
3. Take a boat excursion in the Lauterbrunnen Valley, and experience the waterfalls from a fresh perspective.
4. Go hiking in the neighboring mountains. There are various hiking paths of varied difficulty levels, so you may select one that is ideal for you.
5. Consider riding a cable car to Wengen or Mürren for panoramic views of the Alps
6. Visit the Jungfraujoch, popularly known as the Top of Europe, the highest train station in Europe. From the Jungfraujoch, you can enjoy breathtaking panoramic views of the Swiss Alps. www.jungfrau.ch

Here are some helpful recommendations for arranging your day trip to Lauterbrunnen:

1. The ideal time to visit Lauterbrunnen is during the spring or autumn when the temperature is warm.
2. If you are traveling with children, make sure to see the Trummelbach Falls.

To getl to Lauterbrunnen from Zürich, you may take the railway, however, this train only operates a few times a day. The direct train ride takes roughly 2 hours and 45 minutes. The train leaves from Zürich HB (main railway station) and arrives at Lauterbrunnen station.

The precise instructions are as follows:
- From Zürich HB, take the train to Interlaken Ost.
- Change trains in Interlaken Ost and take the train to Lauterbrunnen.
- The train timetable may be obtained on the Swiss Federal Railways website. website. https://www.sbb.ch/en
- The cost of the railway ticket is roughly 50 Swiss francs (around USD 50).
- Go to the SBB website or app and search for trains from Zürich HB to Lauterbrunnen.
- Choose the train that best meets your schedule and budget.
- Buy your ticket online or at the railway station.
- Go to the platform and wait for your train to arrive.
- Once your train comes, board the train and locate a seat.

Enjoy the journey to Lauterbrunnen!

3. Gruyères: It is a magnificent medieval town in Switzerland, noted for its cheese and its fairytale castle. The town is situated in the canton of Fribourg, approximately a 1.5-hour rail trip from Zürich.

Here are some of the activities you can do in Gruyères:

1. Visit the Gruyères Castle, a historic castle that gives spectacular views of the surrounding landscape.
2. Take a cheese tasting at one of the several cheese manufacturers in town. Gruyères is famed for its cheese, so this is a must-do for every cheese enthusiast! One of the greatest cheese producers in Gruyères is the *La Maison du Gruyère*.

It is situated in the town center, only a short walk from the railway station. The factory provides tours and tastings, and you may even purchase cheese to take home.
The location: Pringy, Pl. de la Gare 3, 1663 Gruyères, Switzerland
Phone: +41 26 921 84 00,
Website: https://www.lamaisondugruyere.ch/

3. Visit the Gruyères Castle and the HR Giger Museum, devoted to the iconic artist behind the "Alien" series.
4. Explore the town's small streets and observe the historic architecture.
5. Enjoy a dinner at one of the numerous restaurants in town, many of which offer classic Swiss cuisine.

To get to Gruyères from Zürich, you may use the train. The trip takes roughly 1.5 hours. The train leaves from Zürich HB (main railway station) and arrives at Gruyères station.
The precise instructions are as follows:
- From Zürich HB, take the train to Bulle.
- Change trains at Bulle and take the train to Gruyères.

The train timetable may be obtained on the Swiss Federal Railways website. Website. https://www.sbb.ch/en
The cost of the train ticket is roughly 40 Swiss francs (around USD 40).
The overall distance is 114 kilometers (71 miles) and the expected travel time is 1 hour and 45 minutes

Here are some helpful recommendations for arranging your day trip to Gruyères:

1. The best time to visit Gruyères is during the spring or autumn when the weather is warm.
2. If you intend on visiting the Gruyères Castle, make sure to get your ticket in advance. The castle may become quite crowded, particularly during high season.

Nearby Historical Towns

1. Baden: Baden, a neighboring historical town in Switzerland. It is a spa town situated in the canton of Aargau, some 25 kilometers (15 miles) north of Zürich.

Baden is a renowned tourist destination, famed for its warm springs, its medieval old town, and its stunning environment. It is recognized as a spa town because it is home to a variety of thermal spas, which have been utilized for generations for their medicinal effects.

The hot water in Baden bubbles out of 18 separate springs, and has a temperature of up to 47°C (117°F). The water is rich in minerals, including calcium, magnesium, and sulfur, which are thought to be good for a range of health concerns.

Here are some of the activities you can do in Baden:

1. Visit the thermal baths: Baden is home to a variety of thermal spas, which have been utilized for generations for their medicinal effects.
- **FORTYSEVEN° Wellness-Therme:** This is the newest thermal bath in Baden, and it is the highlight of the bath area in Baden. It focuses on holistic well-being and features eight indoor and outdoor pools, eleven saunas, and a steam room.

Here is their information:
Address: Grosse Bäder 1, 5400 Baden, Switzerland
Opening hours: Every day from 8 am until 10 pm
Appointments & Menu: fortyseven.ch
Phone: +41 56 269 18 47

- **Novum Spa:** This is a contemporary thermal bath that is situated close to the FORTYSEVEN° Wellness-Therme. It features a variety of pools and saunas, as well as a fitness facility.

Here is their information:
Address: Limmat Promenade 28, 5400 Baden, Switzerland
Phone: +41 56 200 17 17
Appointments & Menu: limmathof.ch

2. **Explore the historic old town:** Baden's old town is a lovely network of tiny streets and lanes, dotted with shops, restaurants, and cafés.

3. **Take a stroll along the river:** The River Limmat passes through Baden, and it's a nice area to take a stroll or a boat trip.

4. **Visit the remnants of the castle:** Baden was previously home to a castle, which was demolished in the 14th century. The remnants of the castle may still be seen today.

5. **Go shopping:** Baden offers a variety of stores providing traditional Swiss souvenirs, as well as fashionable apparel and accessories.

To travel to Baden from Zürich, you may use the train. The trip takes roughly 30 minutes. The train leaves from Zürich HB (main railway station) and arrives at Baden station.
The precise instructions are as follows:
- Take the train from Zürich HB to Baden. The trip takes roughly 30 minutes.
- The train timetable may be obtained on the Swiss Federal Railways website. Website: https://www.sbb.ch/en
- The train leaves from platform 13 or 14 at Zürich HB. It arrives at platform 1 at Baden station.

The train ride is straight and there are no changes necessary.
The cost of the railway ticket is roughly 10 Swiss francs (around USD 10).

The whole distance is 25 kilometers (15 miles) and the expected travel time is 30 minutes.

Here are some helpful recommendations for arranging your day trip to Baden:

1. The greatest time to visit Baden is during the spring or autumn when the weather is warm.
2. If you intend on visiting the thermal baths, make sure to buy your tickets in advance. The baths may become quite crowded, particularly during high season.
3. There are several restaurants in Baden providing traditional Swiss fare. Be sure to taste some of the local favorites.

2. Winterthur: Winterthur, a neighboring town in Switzerland, is a cultural and economic hub situated in the canton of Zürich, some 25 kilometers (15 miles) northeast of Zürich. Winterthur is recognized for its museums, its art scene, and its ancient old town. This cultural center is noted for its art collections, notably the Oskar Reinhart Collection "Am Römerholz" and the Swiss Science Center Technorama. The old town also has ancient buildings and wonderful parks.

Here are some of the activities you can do in Winterthur:

1. Visit the Kunstmuseum Winterthur: The Kunstmuseum Winterthur is one of the most prominent art museums in Switzerland. It holds a collection of nearly 40,000 pieces of art, including paintings, sculptures, and drawings from the Middle Ages to the present day.

2. Explore the historic town: Winterthur's old town is a lovely network of tiny streets and lanes, dotted with stores, restaurants, and cafés.

3. Take a stroll along the river: The River Töss flows through Winterthur, and it's a nice area to take a stroll or a boat trip.

4. Visit the Swiss Transport Museum: The Swiss Transport Museum is a must-see for every transportation aficionado. It holds a collection of nearly 500 vehicles, including trains, automobiles, aircraft, and bicycles.

5. Go shopping: Winterthur features a variety of stores providing traditional Swiss souvenirs, as well as trendy apparel and accessories.

To get to Winterthur from Zürich, you may use the train. The trip takes roughly 20 minutes. The train leaves from Zürich HB (main railway station) and arrives at Winterthur train station.
The precise instructions are as follows:
- Take the train from Zürich HB to Winterthur. The trip takes roughly 20 minutes.
- The train timetable may be obtained on the Swiss Federal Railways website. Website: https://www.sbb.ch/en

The cost of the railway ticket is roughly 6 Swiss francs (around USD 6).
The whole distance is 25 kilometers (15 miles) and the expected travel time is 20 minutes.

Here are some helpful recommendations for arranging your day trip to Winterthur:

1. The greatest time to visit Winterthur is during the spring or autumn when the weather is moderate.

2. If you intend to visit the Kunstmuseum Winterthur, be sure to buy your tickets in advance. The museum may become quite crowded, particularly during high season. The Kunstmuseum

3. Winterthur does not have an official ticket webpage. You may purchase tickets at the museum's ticket office, which is open from 10:00 to 17:00, Tuesday to Sunday. You may also purchase tickets online on the museum's website. https://www.kmw.ch/

4. On the website, click on the "Tickets" option. You will be able to examine the costs of tickets and the various kinds of tickets that are available. You may also order your tickets online.

The pricing of admission to the Kunstmuseum Winterthur is as follows:
Adults: CHF 25
Reduced: CHF 15 (students, pensioners, unemployed, those with impairments)
Free: Children under 16
There are also family tickets available for CHF 55.
I hope you have a nice time in Winterthur!

3. Zug: Zug is a tiny canton situated in Central Switzerland, roughly 30 kilometers (19 miles) southeast of Zürich. Zug is noted for its gorgeous old town, its lakefront position, and its financial services sector. It provides a blend of history and natural beauty.

Here are some of the activities you can do in Zug:

1. Visit the historic town: Zug's old town is a lovely network of tiny streets and lanes, dotted with stores, restaurants, and cafés.

2. Take a stroll near the lake: Lake Zug is a gorgeous lake that is great for a stroll or a boat excursion.

3. Visit the Hofkirche: The Hofkirche is a 15th-century church that is worth a visit for its stunning architecture.

4. **Go shopping:** Zug offers a multitude of stores providing traditional Swiss souvenirs, as well as fashionable garments and accessories.

5. **Enjoy the nightlife:** Zug offers a busy nightlife scene, with a lot of pubs and clubs to pick from.

6. Stroll along the lakefront promenade, tour the lovely old town, and explore Zug Castle.

To travel to Zug from Zürich, you may use the train. The trip takes roughly 30 minutes. The train leaves from Zürich HB (major railway station) and arrives at Zug train station.

The precise instructions are as follows:
- Take the train from Zürich HB to Zug. The trip takes roughly 30 minutes.
- The train timetable may be obtained on the Swiss Federal Railways website: https://www.sbb.ch/en

The cost of the railway ticket is roughly 10 Swiss francs (around USD 10).

The whole distance is 30 kilometers (19 miles) and the expected travel time is 30 minutes.

Here are some more ideas for organizing a day trip to Zug:

1. Zug is best visited in the spring or autumn when the weather is moderate.

2. If you want to visit the Hofkirche, be sure you purchase your tickets in advance. The chapel may get quite crowded, particularly during peak season.

Castles and Ruins

If you're a lover of castles and ruins, Zürich and its surrounding environs offer several intriguing alternatives to explore:

1. **Rapperswil Castle:** Rapperswil Castle Is a medieval castle situated in the town of Rapperswil, Switzerland. It is a renowned tourist site, recognized for its magnificent setting on a rocky promontory overlooking Lake Zürich. The castle was initially erected in the 12th century and has been enlarged and changed throughout the ages. It has been the residence of the Counts of Rapperswil, the Dukes of Württemberg, and the Counts of Toggenburg.
Address: Lindenhügel, 8640 Rapperswil-Jona, Switzerland
Phone: +41 55 210 18 28

The castle is available to the public and provides spectacular views of the lake and the surrounding mountains. There are also a variety of displays about the history of the castle and its prior inhabitants. There is an entry cost to visit Rapperswil Castle.

The pricing is as follows:
- Adults: CHF 10
- Reduced: CHF 8 (students, pensioners, unemployed, those with impairments)
- Free: Children under 6

You may purchase tickets at the castle ticket office, which is open from 10:00 to 17:00, Tuesday to Sunday. You may also purchase tickets online on the castle's website. Here is the link to the castle's website: https://www.schloss-rapperswil.ch/en/.

On the website, click on the "Tickets" option. You will be able to examine the costs of tickets and the various kinds of tickets that are available. You may also order your tickets online.

Here are some of the activities you can do in Rapperswil Castle:

1. Visit the castle museum: The castle museum describes the history of the castle and its past tenants.

2. Take a tour of the castle: There are a variety of tours available, including guided tours and audio tours.

3. Enjoy the sights: The castle provides beautiful views of Lake Zürich and the surrounding Alps.

4. Have a picnic: There is a nice picnic area near the castle.

5. Go on a stroll: There are a variety of walking routes in the vicinity, including a track that climbs to the top of the castle hill. To travel to Rapperswil Castle from Zürich, you may use the train. The trip takes roughly 30 minutes. The train leaves from Zürich HB (major railway station) and arrives at Rapperswil train station.

The precise instructions are as follows:
- Take the train from Zürich HB to Rapperswil. The trip takes roughly 30 minutes.
- The train timetable may be obtained on the Swiss Federal Railways website.
- The train leaves from platform 13 or 14 at Zürich HB. It arrives at platform 1 at Rapperswil railway station.
- The train ride is straight and there are no changes necessary.
- Once you arrive at Rapperswil railway station, follow the signs towards the castle. The castle is situated around a 10-minute walk from the railway station.

The cost of the railway ticket is roughly 10 Swiss francs (around USD 10).
The whole distance is 25 kilometers (15 miles) and the expected travel time is 30 minutes.

Here are some helpful recommendations for arranging your day trip to Rapperswil Castle:

1. The ideal time to visit Rapperswil Castle is during the spring or autumn when the weather is moderate.

2. If you intend to visit the castle museum, make sure to reserve your tickets in advance. The museum may become quite crowded, particularly during high season.

2. Laufen Castle: Laufen Castle is a destroyed castle situated in the town of Laufen, Switzerland. It is a renowned tourist site, recognized for its magnificent setting on a rocky peninsula overlooking the Rhine Falls. The castle was initially erected in the 12th century and was demolished in the 14th century. It has been rebuilt multiple times since then, although it is still regarded to be a ruin.
Address: Areal Schloss Laufen, 8447 Dachsen, Switzerland
Phone: +41 52 659 67 67

The castle is available to the public and provides spectacular views of the Rhine Falls and the surrounding landscape. There are also a variety of displays about the history of the castle and its prior inhabitants. There is an entry cost to visit Laufen Castle.

The pricing is as follows:
- Adults: CHF 5
- Reduced: CHF 3.50 (students, pensioners, unemployed, those with impairments)
- Free: Children under 16

You may purchase tickets at the castle ticket office, which is open from 10:00 to 17:00, Tuesday to Sunday. You may also purchase tickets online on the castle's website. https://www.schlosslaufen.ch/en/

On the website, click on the "Tickets" option. You will be able to examine the costs of tickets and the various kinds of tickets that are available. You may also order your tickets online.

Here are some of the activities you can do at Laufen Castle:

1. Visit the castle museum: The castle museum describes the history of the castle and its past tenants.

2. Take a tour of the castle: There are a variety of tours available, including guided tours and audio tours.

3. Enjoy the sights: The castle provides beautiful views of the Rhine Falls and the surrounding landscape.

4. Have a picnic: There is a nice picnic area near the castle.

5. Go on a stroll: There are a variety of walking routes in the vicinity, including a track that climbs to the top of the castle hill.

To go to Laufen Castle from Zürich, you may use the train. The trip takes roughly 50 minutes. There is no direct rail from Zürich HB to Laufen Castle. You will need to take a train to Schaffhausen, where you will change trains and take a train to Laufen am Rheinfall. The complete trip takes roughly 50 minutes.

Here are the instructions on how to go to Laufen Castle from Zürich HB via train:

- Go to the SBB website or smartphone and search for trains from Zürich HB to Schaffhausen.
- Choose the train that best meets your schedule and budget.
- Buy your ticket online or at the railway station.
- Go to the platform and wait for your train to arrive.

- Once your train comes, board the train and locate a seat.
- The train leaves from platform 13 or 14 at Zürich HB. It arrives at platform 3 at Schaffhausen station.
- Once you arrive at Schaffhausen station, follow the signs for the train to Laufen am Rheinfall.
- The train leaves from platform 2 at Schaffhausen station. It arrives at platform 1 at Laufen am Rheinfall station.

The rail travel from Schaffhausen to Laufen am Rheinfall takes around 10 minutes.

The cost of the railway ticket is roughly 15 Swiss francs (around USD 15).

The whole distance is 35 kilometers (22 miles) and the expected travel time is 50 minutes.

Here are some helpful recommendations for arranging your day trip to Laufen Castle:

1. The ideal time to visit Laufen Castle is during the spring or autumn when the weather is moderate.

2. If you intend to visit the castle museum, make sure to reserve your tickets in advance. The museum may become quite crowded, particularly during high season.

3. Kyburg Castle: Just a short drive from Zürich, Kyburg Castle is set on a hill and gives a fascinating peek into medieval life. Explore its towers, courtyards, and displays. Kyburg Castle is a destroyed castle situated in the municipality of Kyburg, Switzerland. It is a famous tourist site, recognized for its magnificent setting on a rocky promontory overlooking the Aare River. The castle was initially erected in the 11th century and was enlarged and remodeled throughout the ages. It was the home of the Counts of Kyburg, one of the most important houses in Switzerland.

Address: Schloss 1, 8314 Kyburg, Switzerland

Phone: +41 52 232 46 64

The castle was abandoned in the 16th century and has been in ruins ever since. However, it has been painstakingly repaired and is again available to the public. There is an entry cost to visit Kyburg Castle.

- The entry charge is CHF 9 for adults and CHF 5 for youngsters.
- The castle is open from Tuesday through Sunday from 10:30 AM to 5:30 PM.
- You may purchase tickets at the castle ticket office or online https://schlosskyburg.ch/

Here are some of the activities you can do at Kyburg Castle:

1. Visit the castle ruin: The castle ruins provide excellent views of the Aare River and the surrounding landscape.

2. Take a tour of the castle: There are a variety of tours available, including guided tours and audio tours.

3. Enjoy the sights: The castle provides spectacular views of the Aare River and the surrounding landscape.

4. Have a picnic: There is a nice picnic area near the castle.

5. Go on a stroll: There are a variety of walking routes in the vicinity, including a track that climbs to the top of the castle hill.

To travel to Kyburg Castle from Zürich, you may use the train. The trip takes roughly 55 minutes. The train leaves from Zürich HB (main railway station) and arrives at Uerikon station.

There is no direct rail from Zürich HB to Kyburg Castle.

You will need to take a train to Uerikon, where you will change trains and take a bus to Kyburg Castle. The complete trip takes roughly 55 minutes.

Here are the instructions on how to go to Kyburg Castle from Zürich HB via train:

- Go to the SBB website or app and search for trains from Zürich HB to Uerikon.
- Choose the train that best meets your schedule and budget.
- Buy your ticket online or at the railway station.
- Go to the platform and wait for your train to arrive.
- Once your train comes, board the train and locate a seat.
- The train leaves from platform 13 or 14 at Zürich HB. It arrives at platform 2 at Uerikon station.
- Once you arrive at Uerikon station, follow the instructions for the bus to Kyburg Castle.
- The bus leaves from stop 2 at Uerikon station. It arrives at stop 1 at Kyburg Castle.

The bus travel from Uerikon to Kyburg Castle takes around 10 minutes.

The entire cost of the rail and bus tickets is roughly 20 Swiss francs (around USD 20). The whole distance is 35 kilometers (22 miles) and the expected travel time is 45 minutes.

Here are some helpful recommendations for arranging your day trip to Kyburg Castle:

1. The greatest time to visit Kyburg Castle is during the spring or autumn when the weather is warm.

2. If you intend on visiting the castle ruins, make sure to wear comfortable shoes. The ruins may be fairly uneven.

Lake Cruises and Mountain Escape

Here are some of the greatest lake cruises and mountain retreats you can experience in Zürich, Switzerland:

Lake Zürich Boat Cruise: This is a terrific opportunity to explore the city from a new viewpoint and appreciate the gorgeous views of the lake and the surrounding mountains. Various boat companies provide cruises, so you may select one that matches your budget and interests.

Zürichsee Schifffahrt: This is the oldest and biggest boat business in Zürich. They provide a range of cruises, including sightseeing cruises, dinner cruises, and themed cruises. https://www.zsg.ch/en/

Uetliberg Mountain Train: This train takes you up to Uetliberg Mountain, which gives beautiful views of the city and the surrounding region. You may climb, ride, or just enjoy the views from the summit.

Felsenegg: This mountain is situated just outside of Zürich and provides even greater views of the city and the surrounding region than Uetliberg. You may also go hiking, biking, or take the aerial cableway up to the peak.

These are just a handful of the numerous lake cruises and mountain retreats you may experience in Zürich. With so many alternatives to pick from, you're sure to discover the right one for you.

Here are several tour guides who may help you organize your lake cruises and mountain retreats in Zürich, Switzerland, and their websites:

Zürich Tourism: This is the official tourist website of Zürich. They provide a range of trips, including lake cruises, mountain climbs, and city tours. https://www.zuerich.com

Swiss Travel Pass: This is a pass that provides you unlimited travel on all public transportation in Switzerland, including trains, buses, and boats. It may be a terrific way to save money on your lake cruises and mountain retreats. www.sbb.ch

GetYourGuide: This is a website that provides a range of excursions and activities in Zürich, including lake cruises, mountain hikes, and city tours. https://www.getyourguide.com

Viator: This is another website that provides a range of excursions and activities in Zürich, including lake cruises, mountain hikes, and city tours. https://www.viator.com/en-IN/tours/Zürich/Zürich-City-Tour-with-Lake-Cruise/

CHAPTER ELEVEN

SAFETY AND PRACTICAL TIPS

This chapter offers you crucial safety and practical information for your journey to Zürich. Stay safe and enjoy your stay in this wonderful city!

Emergency Contacts

Who can you call in the case of an emergency in Zürich? The list below includes the most significant phone numbers at a glance.

SERVICES	NUMBERS
International emergency number	112
City of Zürich police	117
Fire service	118
Ambulance/Rescue services	144
REGA Swiss Air-Rescue	1414
Toxinfo (in situations of poisoning)	145
Emergency dentist	+41 800 336 655
Emergency doctor & emergency psychiatrist	+41 44 421 21 21
FDFA helpline consular services	+41 800 247 365
The City of Zürich lost property office	+41 800 247 365
Helpline for children & youths	147
Zürich hotline for parents	+41 44 261 88 66
Crisis Intervention Unit (KIZ)	+41 44 296 73 10
Refuge for girls	+41 44 341 49 45

Local Laws and Customs

Here are some of the local rules and practices of Zürich that first-time visitors and tourists should know:

1. Be mindful of the drinking rules: The legal drinking age in Switzerland is 16 years old. However, it is forbidden to consume alcohol in public locations, such as on the streets or in parks.

2. Be respectful of the local culture: Switzerland is a relatively conservative nation, thus it is necessary to be respectful of local customs and traditions. For example, it is considered disrespectful to point with your finger.

3. Learn a few simple phrases in German: While English is commonly spoken in Zürich, it is always appreciated when tourists make an effort to acquire a few simple phrases in German. This will indicate that you are attempting to appreciate the local culture.

4. Be cognizant of the clothing code: Switzerland is a formal nation, therefore it is vital to dress correctly. This means no shorts, tank tops, or flip-flops in most public locations.

5. Be conscious of the tipping norms: Tipping is not required in Switzerland however, it is welcomed in specific instances, such as in restaurants. A little gratuity of roughly 10% is considered normal.

6. Be mindful of the public transit system: Zürich has an outstanding public transit system, so it is simple to travel about without a vehicle. The Swiss Travel Pass is a terrific way to save money on public transportation.

7. Be mindful of the funds in your possession: The Swiss currency is the Swiss franc (CHF). You may swap your currency at most banks and currency exchange agencies.

8. Be mindful of the weather: The weather in Zürich may vary fast, therefore it is necessary to be prepared for all sorts of weather circumstances. The summers are bright and sunny, while the winters are chilly and snowy.

9. Be careful of the noise rules: It is unlawful to generate excessive noise in residential areas, such as playing music loudly or yelling.
10. Be mindful of the recycling rules: Switzerland has a highly stringent recycling policy, thus it is necessary to recycle your garbage appropriately.
11. Be careful of the littering rules: Littering is forbidden in Zürich, thus it is necessary to dispose of your rubbish appropriately.
12. Be prudent of the jaywalking regulations: Jaywalking is forbidden in Zürich, hence it is vital to cross the street at specified crosswalks.
13. Be careful of the speed limitations The speed restrictions in Zürich are severely enforced, thus it is necessary to follow them.
14. Be careful of the pedestrian's right of way: Pedestrians have the right of way in Zürich, thus it is vital to defer to them while crossing the street.
15. Be conscious of public transportation etiquette: It is crucial to be courteous and thoughtful while utilizing public transit in Zürich. This involves giving up your seat to the elderly and handicapped, and not chatting on your phone loudly.
16. Be conscious of the cultural differences: Switzerland is a cosmopolitan nation, thus it is necessary to be tolerant of diverse cultures. This includes avoiding forming assumptions about someone based on their looks or background.
17. Be mindful of the emergency services: If you need assistance, phone 112 for the emergency services.
18. Be careful of the water fountain etiquette: It is usual in Zürich to drink from public water fountains. However, it is necessary to be courteous and not squander water.
19. Be conscious of the queueing culture: The Swiss are highly tidy people, thus it is vital to line up while waiting for items, like public transit or to enter a business.
20. Be cognizant of the gift-giving norms: It is not usual to send gifts to your hosts in Switzerland. However, if you do want to offer a present, it is ideal to provide something little and considerate.

Staying Safe While Traveling

Here are some recommendations for being safe when going to Zürich:

1. Be alert of your surroundings and take measures against pickpockets: Pickpocketing is a widespread issue in tourist places, therefore it is crucial to be aware of your surroundings and take measures. Keep your valuables close to you, and do not flaunt them around.

2. Don't leave valuables unattended: It is also vital to not leave valuables unattended, even for a few minutes. This includes your handbag, wallet, phone, and other items.

3. Be careful of the weather, particularly during the winter months: The weather in Zürich may vary fast, therefore it is necessary to be prepared for all sorts of weather circumstances. The summers are bright and sunny, while the winters are chilly and snowy.

4. Drink lots of water, particularly if you are coming during the heat: The air in Zürich may be dry, therefore it is necessary to drink enough water to remain hydrated.

5. Respect local norms and traditions: Switzerland is a relatively conservative nation, thus it is necessary to be respectful of local customs and traditions. For example, it is considered disrespectful to point with your finger.

6. Stay in well-lit locations at night: Avoid wandering alone in dark or desolate regions, particularly at night.

7. Be alert of your surroundings while utilizing public transit: Keep your belongings near to you, and do not fall asleep on the train or bus.

8. Don't show your cash or valuables: This will draw unwelcome attention from criminals.

9. Be cautious while using cabs: Make careful you utilize legal taxis and only pay the fee displayed on the meter.

10. Report any suspicious behavior to the police: If you see anything, say something.

11. Be careful of the frauds that are popular in tourist locations: For example, be aware of persons who offer to assist you with your baggage or who attempt to sell you imitation items.

12. Get travel insurance: This will safeguard you financially in case of any accidents or theft.

13. Stay updated about the current security dangers: You may accomplish this by monitoring the news and reading travel warnings.

14. Use common sense: Trust your gut sense and don't do anything that makes you feel uncomfortable.

15. Use a money belt or other safe means to carry your passport and other critical papers.

16. Be cautious while using ATMs, particularly in unfamiliar regions.

17. Don't take beverages or food from strangers.

18. Trust your intuition. If you feel unsafe, leave the situation.

By following these guidelines, you may help guarantee a safe and pleasurable vacation to Zürich.

Communication Tips

Here are some communication guidelines in Zürich for first-time visitors and tourists to know:

1. The official language of Switzerland is German. However, English is commonly spoken in Zürich, so you should be able to get by without knowing any German.

2. Be conscious of the cultural variations in communicating. For example, it is considered disrespectful to point with your finger in Switzerland.

3. Be patient. The Swiss are renowned for being straightforward and efficient, so it may take some time to become adjusted to their communication style.

4. Don't be hesitant to ask for assistance. If you are struggling to communicate, don't hesitate to seek assistance from a local.
Here are some extra tips:

5. Use a translating app. There are various translation applications available that may help you communicate with folks who speak different languages.

6. Learn some fundamental gestures. Several gestures may be used to communicate without speaking.

7. Be prepared to write things down. If you find it difficult to communicate vocally, you may need to write things down.

8. Don't be frightened to make errors. Everyone makes errors while they are learning a new language.

By following these recommendations, you can help guarantee that your conversation in Zürich is seamless and pleasurable.

Basic German Expressions

If you wish to learn any German, it is valued by the locals. Here are some fundamental words that you may learn:

ENGLISH	GERMAN
Hello or Hallo	Grüß Gott
Goodbye	Auf Wiedersehen
Thank you	Danke
You're welcome	Bitte
Excuse me	Entschuldigung
Do you speak English?	Sprechen Sie Englisch?
How are you?	Wie geht es dir?
I'm fine	Mir geht es gut
What is your name?	Wie ist dein Name?
My name is…	Ich heiße…
Where are you from?	Woher kommst du?
I'm from…	Ich bin aus…
Do you like Zürich?	Magst du Zürich?
Yes, I do	Ja, ich mag es
No, I don't	Nein, ich mag es nicht
Can you help me?	Kannst du mir helfen?
I need help	Ich brauche Hilfe
Where is the bathroom?	Wo ist die Toilette?
Where's the nearest restaurant?	Wo ist das nächste Restaurant?
How much does this cost?	Was kostet das?
Can I have a receipt?	Kann ich eine Quittung haben?
I'm lost	Ich bin verloren
Can you call a taxi for me?	Kannst du mir ein Taxi rufen?
I'm sorry	Es tut mir leid
Please	Bitte
Thank you very much	Vielen Dank
You're welcome very much	Sehr gerne
Nice to meet you	Schön dich kennenzulernen
See you later	Bis später
Have a good day	Hab einen schönen Tag
Have a good trip	Gute Reise

CONCLUSION

Congratulations on completing the Zürich Travel Guide! I hope you find this book useful in arranging your visit to this lovely city.

This book addressed a wide range of topics, from Zürich's history and culture to the greatest locations to dine, buy, and sightseeing. I've also added some interesting facts and trivia about the city to assist you in learning more about it.

Of course, no travel guide would be complete without some useful tips. Everything from getting about Zürich to where to stay and what to carry was addressed.

So, whether you're a first-time visitor or an experienced traveler, I hope this book has provided you with the knowledge you need to arrange a memorable vacation to Zürich.

It's time to say goodbye to Zürich now that you've read the book. I hope you have a nice experience in the city and that you will return shortly.

Please share your trip experiences with me on Facebook (Christine M. Edmonson) or by email (edmonsonchristine@gmail.com) in the interim. I'd love to hear about your exploits!

Check out our other travel guides as well. We provide guides to all kinds of great destinations all around the globe.

Finally, we'd appreciate it if you could write us a review of the Zürich Travel Guide. Your input helps us to improve our guides even further.
Thank you for taking the time to read this!

Appendix

Useful Websites and Resources

Zürich tourism: https://www.Zürich.com/en/ - Zürich's official tourist website. This website has a variety of information on things to see and do in Zürich, as well as trip-planning advice.

Swiss Travel System: https://www.swissrailways.com/ - The Swiss national railway company's website. This website allows you to plan rail trips in Switzerland and offers Swiss Rail passes.

Rome2Rio: https://www.rome2rio.com/ - A website for planning transportation routes between any two cities in the globe.

City-mapper: A transit app that displays real-time arrival information for Zürich public transportation.

SBB Mobile: The Swiss Federal Railways' official app. This software lets you plan rail trips, purchase tickets, and monitor your train in real-time.

Swiss Federal Railways website: Pass provides unlimited travel on trains, buses, and boats throughout Switzerland. https://www.sbb.ch/en

Uber: A taxi service that may be utilized to travel about Zürich.

Lyft: Another ride-hailing app for getting about Zürich.

Moovit: A public transportation app that displays real-time arrival information for Zürich and other cities across the globe.

XE Currency Converter: This software converts currencies so you always know how much your money is worth in Swiss francs.

Google Translate: This program can translate text and voice between over 100 languages, allowing you to converse with Zürich residents.

The Local: An English-language website and app that delivers news and information about Zürich.

Zürich Card: A city card that allows you to visit several museums and sites in Zürich for free, as well as get savings on public transit and other activities.

Swiss Travel Pass Flex: A more flexible version of the Swiss Rail Pass that enables you to travel on certain dates throughout the month.

Printed in Great Britain
by Amazon